Inquiry-Based Early Learning Environments

INQUIRY-BASED EARLY LEARNING ENVIRONMENTS

Creating, Supporting, and Collaborating

SUSAN STACEY

Redleaf Press®
www.redleafpress.org
800-423-8309

Published by Redleaf Press
10 Yorkton Court
St. Paul, MN 55117
www.redleafpress.org
© 2019 Susan Stacey

Cover design by Erin Kirk New
Cover photograph by Mahony-stock.adobe.com
Interior design by Michelle Lee Lagerroos
Typeset in Adobe Caslon Pro, Myriad Pro, Jubilat, Haboro Soft, and
    Moonlight
Interior photos/illustrations by Susan Stacey; Debi Keyte-Hartland; Offering
    Invitations, London Bridge 2016
"Loose Parts and Intelligent Playthings Categorized by Schema" © 2015 by
    Michelle Thornhill. Reprinted with permission.
Printed in the United States of America
25 24 23 22 21 20 19 18   1 2 3 4 5 6 7 8

Library of Congress Cataloging-in-Publication Data
Names: Stacey, Susan, author.
Title: Inquiry-based early learning environments : creating, supporting, and
    collaborating / Susan Stacey.
Description: St. Paul, MN : Redleaf Press, 2018. | Includes bibliographical
    references and index.
Identifiers: LCCN 2018008012 (print) | LCCN 2018023494 (ebook) | ISBN
    9781605545820 (ebook) | ISBN 9781605545813 (pbk. : alk. paper)
Subjects: LCSH: Reggio Emilia approach (Early childhood education) |
    Inquiry-based learning.
Classification: LCC LB1139.23 (ebook) | LCC LB1139.23 .S727 2018 (print) |
    DDC 372.21--dc23
LC record available at https://lccn.loc.gov/2018008012

Printed on acid-free paper

For my father, Lewis, who throughout his entire life demonstrated a deep and lively curiosity about how the world works and passed this curiosity on to his children so that we, too, have become lifelong learners. With much love and gratitude.

Contents

Acknowledgments

Many people have contributed their thoughts, experiences, and practical assistance to complete this book and make it richer. It is my belief that their stories of challenges and successes will make the topic of inquiry come to life for readers and nurture the belief that this type of approach can and does happen in early years settings—and that it indeed brings joy to children's learning and passion to the teaching experience.

The generosity of colleagues within our profession continues to astound me. The team members at London Bridge Child Care Services in London, Ontario, were willing to share thoughts around their mission and how they make it come to life, as well as photographs that exemplify their practices. Similarly, educators and leaders at Madeley Nursery School in the United Kingdom and the directors at Prospect Bay Children's Centre (Lynda Noble), Small World Learning Centre (Donna Stapleton), Forest Kids (Terri Kottwitz), and Point Pleasant Child Care Centre (Susan Willis) all willingly shared photographs and experiences.

The teaching team introduced in the last chapter of this book deserve special mention. S. J., Aya, and B. not only shared their work but also their vulnerability, which takes courage.

There are examples in this book from far-off places such as Beijing, thanks to international consultant Debi Keyte-Hartland, and from the far north of Canada (Sioux Lookout), where teachers demonstrated the value of dedicated self-directed study when I visited them last year.

My own learning over several decades has been enriched by thinking alongside some great minds. The Emergent Curriculum group in Halifax, Nova Scotia, has been a source of much discourse, provocations, wondering, and growth. I have also learned that "thinking online" with colleagues is almost as satisfying as talking face-to-face! In this way, I have been in conversation regularly over the years with those whom I only meet up with occasionally: the wonderful and provocative thinker Elizabeth Jones, Laurel Fynes, Julie Mann-Harrison, and all those educators who share their thinking through blogs and online articles. It takes time and energy to share in this way, and dozens of our colleagues take the time to do it.

Closer to home, I am privileged to have the opportunity to converse with Dr. Carol Anne Wien, Liz Hicks, Janette March, Carrie Melsom, and Annette Comeau, all of whom allow me to try out my sometimes tentative ideas with them.

I must offer profound gratitude to the educators of Reggio Emilia, who have shared their work in so many ways with the rest of the world's early years educators. While this book is not about them, it reflects the level of inspiration they have provided for us over the years. For some of us, they have been a catalyst that has moved us to deep reflection about our own practices and how to make our values visible.

I thank the editors at Redleaf Press, particularly Cathy Broberg, whose questions, reminders, and inquiries provoked me, in many cases, to a clearer explanation of this type of teaching practice. Finally, thanks to my family—near and far—who listen to my endless thinking about why we do what we do in early education, my joys and frustrations, and my hopes and aspirations. Thank you to my loved ones for listening.

Introduction: The Quest for Knowledge

What does it mean to inquire? In our everyday lives, we might think of inquiry as questioning, searching for information, or finding out about a topic we are interested in. For children in their early years classrooms, the definition is no different—from the time of their birth, they want to know how the world works and are on a quest to actively search out information. How we as educators might best respond to this quest is what this book is about. How do children's questions and ideas affect our practice? Our classroom environments? Our relationships with children? How do we provide environments that support inquiry?

Within this book, I use the term *environment* in a way that encompasses many aspects. At first we may tend to think of environment as a physical space, and, of course, it is. Yet it is also so much more. We can also consider the environment as a place where we respond to provocations, the unusual, and the puzzling. We can think of it as a space that intrigues us to move in new directions and as a setting where relationships are formed, decisions are made, and a particular culture—a way of being—might be formed. What if this culture was one where children's questions are expected, valued by their teachers and community, and taken seriously enough that their ideas are put into action? Where teachers consider their own questions as well as those that come from the children, even if this causes a change of plan or takes them in an unexpected direction? What difference would this make to our daily practice? Throughout this book, we too will be on a quest—a quest to consider how inquiry, in all its forms, might open our eyes to a broader, deeper teaching practice.

Many Forms of Inquiry: What Does It Look Like in Practice?

Inquiry has the potential to be a "messy" practice. For children, it is messy in the sense that they need to get their hands on materials and their minds on ideas to mess about, make mistakes, revisit, and repeat many times. For

adults the cycle is pretty much the same. In our collaboration with children, we also should be familiar with the materials so we understand their possibilities; we can only do that through trial and error, messing about and experimenting with possibilities until we understand how a particular material or process works.

In our thinking—which might also feel a little confused or messy if we are in unfamiliar territory—we can expect to sometimes be unsure, to take a step forward without really knowing where it will lead us, and, in time, to be comfortable with the disequilibrium that this may cause. We can also expect to be wrong sometimes (for instance, when we misunderstand children's intentions or thinking) and to use our stumbles as a way to dig deeper and learn more about the children's ideas. We can revisit, think again, and repeat.

Inquiry can take many forms, and perhaps one of the most familiar and comfortable for us as educators is that of hands-on exploration of materials. This means we explore them to find out how they work, the effect they have, how they can be combined, and what possibilities exist for their use. For instance, a material such as clay might be used in combination with

What Is Messing About?

David Hawkins is an educator whose life bridges the boundaries between scientist and philosopher, teacher and writer, scholar and activist. For more than two decades he has helped to bring teaching and curriculum materials in tune with the ways in which children learn.

—Thomas James, "Teacher of Teachers, Companion of Children"

Educators David Hawkins and his wife, Frances, directed the Mountain View Center for Environmental Education in Boulder, Colorado. He referred to children as curious, active investigators who were willing to take risks, and he felt that teachers could learn about teaching in the same way: by being curious, risk-taking investigators. Referring to professional learning for teachers, Hawkins remarked that it is "something to which the advisors and teachers must participate equally. Exploration, invention, experimentation—but not training as though the trainer knew beforehand what the trainee should do."

At the Boulder Journey School, the influence of David and Frances Hawkins and the work taking place in Reggio Emilia, Italy, has been profound. The leaders at Boulder Journey School, who also mentor student teachers in their program, developed the Hawkins Room for messing about with materials and ideas. They state, "We envisioned a room that would challenge teachers to broaden their understandings of scientific concepts and wondered how this might impact the learning taking place in our classrooms" (Lynch, Schaffer, and Hall 2009).

The term *messing about* has become an important one in the early childhood vernacular, one that describes hands-on learning with materials, for adults, that will ultimately benefit the children in their classrooms.

Cycle of Inquiry for Both Children and Adults

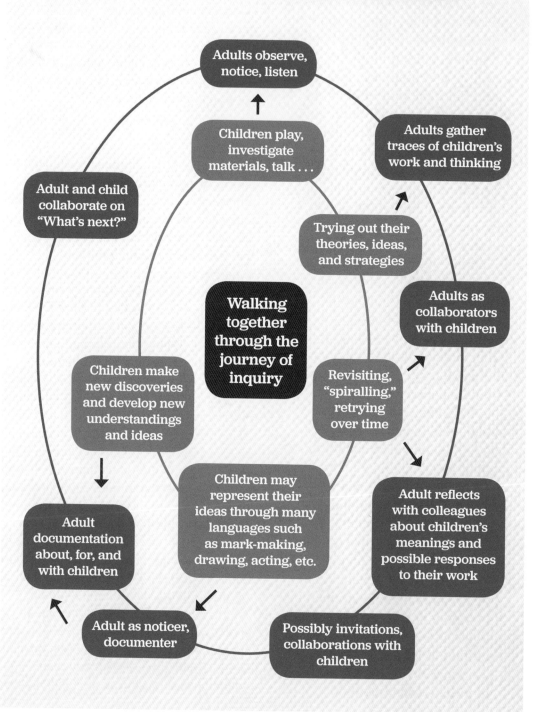

something else, giving not only an unusual effect but also a different use. We will explore the use of materials in some depth in a later chapter, but here is a first example, involving natural materials:

Having observed children watching birds for some time and then asking questions about trees, it came as no surprise to teachers when this group of four-year-olds wanted to build a tree house in their classroom. Providing branches, sections of tree trunks, burlap, and lots of tape enabled these children to construct an indoor tree house by themselves. This was their own design, built over a period of two weeks with lots of trial and error and no assistance from adults, except for occasional encouragement.

Here we see that children have used clay not as a sculpting medium but as a tool. Wanting to make their sticks stand upright and having had many experiences with clay, they were able to see this medium's possibilities for helping them achieve their goal.

Inquiry might also appear as pure experimentation. This could connect with children's questions about how the world works. To find out, the child watches and often experiments with replicating a process. A toddler, for instance, might be fascinated with the disappearance of water down a sink and will experiment for long periods of time (if allowed!) with turning the faucet on and off, peering underneath the sink, or playing for hours at the water table. Preschoolers or kindergartners are often curious about print and how it works. They are surrounded by it, realize its importance in the world (because adults use it all the time), and begin to experiment. We see scribbles, symbols, lines, and forms arranged intentionally on the page as these emerging writers experiment with "what works" in terms of being understood.

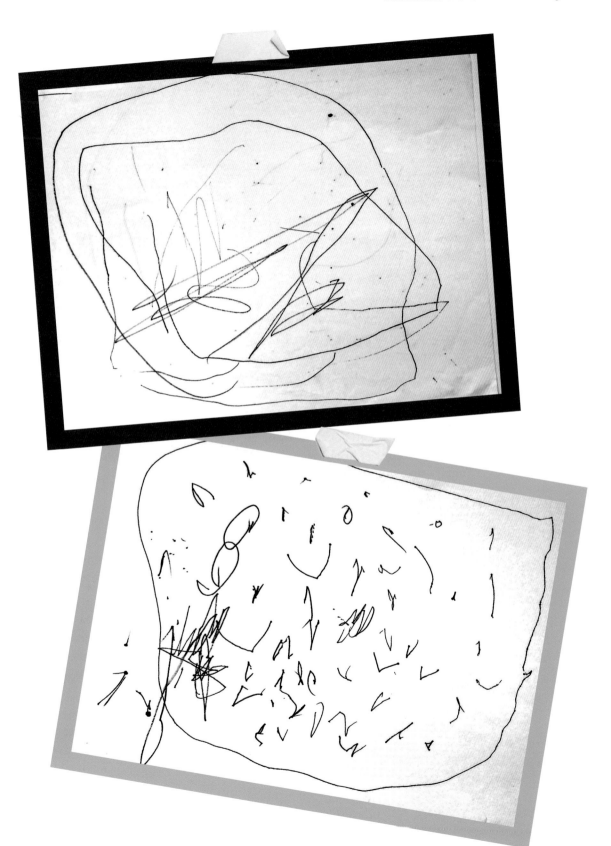

And we should not forget that inquiry often involves revisiting what has already been attempted. It is helpful for all of us—adults and children alike—to revisit past attempts when we are learning something new. What worked? What didn't? Why? Even the youngest child will have something to say, or demonstrate body language that sends a message, when revisiting a photograph of their play or work. To see a visual representation of what we did helps us think through what happened, what we enjoyed, what was frustrating, and what we might do about that. Having a conversation with an educator or more proficient peer while looking at photographs means that the child may then try to articulate what happened. Again this leads to deeper thinking, a kind of cementing of children's provisional theories.

When we think about ways to support inquiry, then, it's also helpful to keep the benefits of doing so in mind:

- First, in early years settings, inquiry is based in play. This means that in an environment that already puts a high value on play, inquiry is already present and providing rich opportunities for us to explore. There are no major changes, therefore, in philosophy when we work to support inquiry, only an enhanced "noticing and responding" that needs to happen.

- For those engaged in emergent curriculum, inquiry is a natural outcome of deep engagement. For those using more prescriptive approaches (for instance, within a school system), there is the opportunity to introduce inquiry that will "loosen up" some old scripts while still staying within required frameworks.

- We know that children are biologically wired to learn. Within play and inquiry, children can also learn how to learn. This is quite different from traditional approaches, where a top-down method (that is, a method that views the teacher as holder and transmitter of knowledge) contains little meaning for young children.

- Just about any skill can arise and be developed within inquiry. There is opportunity for problem solving, collaboration, literacy, math, science, artistic expression, and so on, all at the child's own level. Rather than follow a script or checklist, we follow the ideas and theories of children and then notice the skills and learning taking place within the inquiry. They will be there! At times there will be naturally arising opportunities to scaffold these skills, giving the educator an opportunity to collaborate with children individually or in small groups.

- As children learn to tackle challenges (which will inevitably arise), self-confidence builds, as does the ability to collaborate and think together.

Play as Inquiry

When we play, as children or as adults, we explore, wonder, and investigate. We try out varied ways of doing things and adapt our approaches. As humans we are constantly playing with new ideas and strategies, and we learn from this play—this is discovery through playing with ideas. What's more, we have fun doing it; we are motivated to continue with play, as we find it interesting and engaging.

Elizabeth Jones and Gretchen Reynolds (1992, 1), authors of *The Play's the Thing*, describe what happens during play:

> Master players are skilled at representing their experiences symbolically in self-initiated improvisational drama. Sometimes alone, sometimes in collaboration with others, they play out their fantasies and the events of their daily lives. Through pretend play young children consolidate their understanding of the world, their language, and their social skills. The skillful teacher of young children is one who makes such play possible and helps children keep getting better at it.

In the video *Play*, Dr. Peter Gray and Sir Ken Robinson (2015), both advocates of play in the lives of children, address the idea of imaginative thinking that develops through play, stating that "geniuses seem to be those who retain into adulthood the imaginative capacities of young children."

We see imagination come to life in our everyday work with young children, and we commonly observe young children who are so captured by their play experiences that they are "in their own world" and do not see or hear what is going on around them. Similarly, if adults allow themselves to play as children do, perhaps with new ideas or approaches, they enter into a state of what Mihaly Csikszentmihalyi refers to as "flow," a very satisfying state which is both alert and calm (1996).

In his TEDx Jerusalem talk, "Living in a Playful Collage," Hanoch Piven (2012), an artist who uses everyday objects in creative and playful ways, points out that play leads to creativity and to looking at the world in a different way. He compares the direct versus the playful path, noting that "off the main road, we find treasures . . . playfulness lets you make mistakes," which allows for adaptation and flexibility.

As educators of young children, we are so fortunate to be working with those who see the world in flexible, adaptable, and unusual ways. Through their play, children remind us to really see, with wide-open eyes, all possibilities. At this point in their lives, they have few preconceptions about how to use materials or how to approach a challenge or play out their thinking—they simply dive in and try out their big ideas. In a supportive environment, they are fearless in their explorations.

Within the following chapters, we'll explore all the ways that we can think about the terms *environment* and *inquiry* as well as how these ideas might affect our daily practice and the children and teachers who collaborate in learning together.

How to Use This Book

In chapter 2, we will examine physical environments and our play spaces (indoors and outside), and how these spaces affect both children and adults. These are the spaces that belong to us all where we think, learn, and collaborate together with children. We will take a look at interesting materials that are out of the ordinary and encourage exploration and creativity. We'll also explore the role of time and aesthetics.

Chapter 3 addresses the idea of risk taking. While we all strive to keep children physically and emotionally safe, we must also provide an environment where it is safe to take a risk with our thinking. We will consider the role of disequilibrium in our daily practice and how this can be a benefit rather than a discomfort. We will also take a look at the outdoor curriculum in Denmark, where children are outside for most of the day, in all types of weather, and see some examples of projects from North America as well.

A culture of curiosity and questioning is considered in chapter 4, where we explore how our own curiosity about what children are doing can enrich our practices. We will hear from educators who actually interview prospective teachers for the disposition of curiosity and whose mission statements include the role of curiosity. How can we develop curriculum from curiosity and questioning? Two projects will be examined to demonstrate how this might be achieved.

Chapter 5 takes a look at environments that make thinking visible through documentation. It is possible, with documentation as a type of conduit, to pull inquiry, reflection, and practice together in a way that the reader is able to understand. In this chapter, we will see examples from North America (Canada and the United States) and from Beijing, China.

Chapter 6 considers environments that support teachers' growth, which in turn affects children. Professional learning is also examined. What do we need as teachers to encourage our growth toward inquiry-based practices? What support systems need to be in place? This chapter provides answers to help guide us.

In chapter 7, we will think about environments that support and nurture relationships. What kinds of differences do relationships make in our classrooms? We will examine not only relationships between people but also those between people and materials, as well as the types of places within our classrooms where materials can be used freely by children. The atelier, as exemplified by schools in Reggio Emilia, is examined along with the role of documentation as we reach out to families and the wider community.

At the end of chapters 1 through 7, there will be a section called "Something to Try," an invitation to put to use those ideas you have been reading about. It is my hope that through these invitations, educators will take a step into inquiry, both for themselves as teachers exploring different ways of being in the classroom and for the children, who will lead the way in this journey of discovery.

The book will close with chapter 8, which offers a thorough example of three teachers supporting inquiry in their classroom. This inquiry, which was confusing and sometimes troubling for the educators, demonstrates exemplary practice undertaken by somewhat novice teachers who were able to trust in the process and move forward into an in-depth and unusual inquiry with their children. Their deep reflections and the insights they gained remind us that moving into uncharted territory is often worth the disequilibrium!

Finally we will consider some closing thoughts from which you can move forward in your practice with confidence and curiosity.

Setting the Stage for Inquiry: The Physical Environment

Setting up an environment that entices us to think and work together with children begins with a space. In our profession, it is not usually a perfect space and often has to be adapted to suit the learning styles of young children. Yet even in a purpose-built "ideal" space, there are many facets to take into consideration before we place even one item. First and foremost, who and what is this space for? The answer to this may seem obvious, but the fact is that many early years spaces seem to have adult needs at the forefront.

Imagine emptying your present classroom and beginning over again. We might ask ourselves the following questions: Who does this space belong to? How is this made visible? Do the children have a point of view about how this space might be used? If they are nonverbal, how might they demonstrate their ideas about using space?

Belonging to All the Protagonists

If you believe that the space belongs as much to the children as it does to adults—that both have a right to feel a sense of comfort, freedom, and efficiency within the space—then what has to happen in terms of practical action and our thinking about environments? How will the space reflect our values and beliefs, as well as the children's needs?

I have been fortunate, on four occasions, to have the privilege of setting up a brand-new environment. Here are some things I learned along the way:

- Keep your ideals and philosophy and those of your organization in mind at all times. For instance, if a guiding philosophy includes valuing the child's independence, what will this look like in the physical setup?

- Use what you have. Perhaps you have wonderful natural light in one area of the room. What kind of play or investigation would benefit from this light?

- Examine old scripts of "what should be" in an early childhood education (ECE) environment. If you are familiar with the children who will play and learn in this room, ask yourself what *they* need.

- Is there a space for children to "just be"? A quiet place for wonder?

In an existing environment, it is important to stand back and watch closely as children play. In a space that has ample choice of materials, we can watch for what children *actually do* with the materials (not what we intended them to do, or what we thought they might do, but what actually happens!), how they move from one area to another, the types of things that they gravitate toward, and the things they ignore. What do these actions tell us? Over time these actions upon the environment will change depending upon the children's growth, thinking, and ideas. It is important to keep watching and adapting, providing for flexibility, and responding to how the environment is put to use—no matter how unusual the children's ideas may be.

What Is a Protagonist?

In an early years setting, a *protagonist* is one who takes an active role in learning. In an inquiry-based, emergent setting, this would include the child, teachers, and families. This term conveys equal participation and belief in the child as being strong, capable, and competent.

After displaying a continued interest in birds and nests, a few children one day spontaneously began tallying the number of birds that appeared at the bird feeder outside their classroom. Teachers had already provided "reading baskets" (that is, laundry baskets used as a cozy place to read) and now invited children to sit comfortably in these, in the reading space, to watch the birds from the best vantage point. This concentrated and somewhat peaceful observation by children led to a discussion of why the birds liked this feeder and an inquiry into what kinds of food they enjoyed most.

One of the areas where we need to apply caution is that of scripts. A *script* in the context of our profession is a widely held view of how things are done or how things should be. The problem with scripts is that they can become stale, preventing us from applying other lenses or ways of being in our workplace. Therefore we should be looking at our environments regularly through fresh eyes.

This is sometimes difficult to do for adults because we are so entrenched in scripts, not only ones imposed upon ourselves from our previous learning or experiences, but also those coming from our regulatory bodies (such as

What Are Scripts?

Scripts refer to long-held ways of doing things, and we use them in all walks of life for whatever we are doing in everyday circumstances. For instance, scripts exist for how to put together a report or how to get to work and back. In other words, scripts allow us to go on automatic pilot and not have to think consciously about every little thing that we undertake in daily life.

Similarly, scripts exist in education and are very powerful. We learn in preservice training, for instance, how circle times should be enacted or how curriculum should be developed in advance. What these long-held scripts do not address, however, are the ideas, dispositions, and capabilities of children. When we reexamine old scripts, we ask ourselves why we are practicing in a certain way and make adjustments. When we respond to children after really listening and watching, we can break old scripts and step forward into a more engaging and meaningful practice (Stacey 2011).

licensing or school boards). Yet we can be creative in how we work with regulations and meet requirements in entirely new ways.

The educators in Reggio Emilia, Italy, have given us many examples of how we might think about environments in different ways. Some examples include using tiers for group gatherings instead of chairs or mats, providing a rolling art cart instead of an "art center" so that materials can be used in many parts of the classroom, or using the outdoor patio as a wonderful spread-out space for loose parts.

If we think about breaking scripts, we are working toward an environment that is flexible, responsive, and workable for *everyone* in the classroom. Working in this type of space can be transformative, for when we work in a different, interesting, and perhaps provocative type of physical space, the possibility of thinking in a different way opens up.

In *Inspiring Spaces for Young Children*, the authors discuss how to find inspiration within our physical spaces:

> To begin to understand the principles of designing beautiful classroom spaces, you must learn to search for what inspires and excites you. Your inspiration may come from a visit to a nearby paint store. Looking at paint chips and browsing the brochures that show how colors work together might spark an idea for a new look for your classroom. Or, the color scheme of a beautifully embroidered pillow that you bought for fifty cents at a yard sale may be your inspiration. Try looking beyond the early childhood catalogue and flip through some home decorating catalogues . . . visit a home store or go to an art gallery. Spend a sunny day at the local nursery or lumber yard. Walk through a resale shop. Borrow your inspiration from anywhere. (DeViney et al. 2010)

While the use of color will, of course, affect the ambience of the room, so will the placement of furniture and what kind of furniture we might use. Items don't have to be intended for children; interesting pieces can be reused in creative ways by simply repainting them, turning them upside down (an old table turned into a four-poster doll's bed, perhaps?), or finding a completely different purpose for the pieces. Given the opportunity, the children themselves are likely to be very good at this!

This creative approach applies to outdoor as well as indoor environments, as we see here:

Materials That Entice and Engage

When we have decided how furniture and areas will be arranged in our space, taking into account such practicalities as visibility and traffic flow, how do we decide what types of materials will be best suited for inquiry by this particular group of children? The choices we make about materials should be intentional rather than the rote thinking that goes along with "this is what an early childhood classroom should look or be like."

Instead let's broaden our perspective and think about the kinds of things that children of all ages want to know: How does the world work? How can I find out? What does this thing do? As you form relationships with your particular group of children, there naturally will be specific investigations and small moments that you will need to respond to with materials.

But if we imagine that it is September and you are with a new group of children that you don't know very well just yet, what kinds of things might be intriguing for them to use? Here are some possibilities to consider.

Materials That Reflect Their Lives and Cultures

When someone enters your early childhood setting, how do they know where they are? Apart from photographs that may appear within your documentation, what other artifacts and materials reflect the children's culture, life experiences, and the larger communities that surround them? These days we are used to great diversity within our classrooms, and certainly all children should see themselves and their cultures represented.

At Prospect Bay Children's Centre, in Nova Scotia, Canada, the program emphasis is on the outdoors, the fishing community that surrounds this center and its families, and caring for the environment. How does this appear in everyday life and play? In the large outdoor space, a boat is embedded into the ground as an invitation to play out family members' work lives, there are viewing "windows" in the wooden fence so that children can see the larger forest—and its creatures!—beyond the fence, and loose parts (mostly recycled) are abundant. It is easy to understand something of the philosophy of this center when watching how children respond to this space.

Materials That Provide for Movement from Simple to Complex Play

The idea of simple and complex materials first appeared in 1969 in *Planning Environments for Young Children* by Sybil Kritchevsky, Elizabeth Prescott, and Lee Walling. They described the idea of simple, complex, and super units in reference to play materials. More recently, Prescott (2008, 35) again explained this concept in the practical sense:

> Play equipment can differ in its holding power, i.e., the capacity to sustain attention. We have called this dimension complexity and have rated play units according to the number of different materials which are combined. A simple unit has one manipulable aspect, a complex unit has two different kinds of materials combined, and a super unit has three different kinds of materials that go together.

For example, a sand pile with no equipment is a simple unit. Add digging equipment and it is a complex unit. If you add water as a third element, it becomes a super unit. Playdough by itself is a simple unit. With toothpicks it is a complex unit, and with toothpicks and cookie cutters it is a super unit.

We would do well to keep this seminal work from 1969 in mind as we consider materials for this day and age. How many of our materials actually allow children to explore and engage at deeper and deeper levels as they continue to play? Or, in contrast, do most of our materials allow for only one type of play, idea, or investigation? How likely are our children to remain engaged with such a material? Here is an example of how a simple play material can become more complex as we observe children and perceive their need for further depth and exploration:

Children were playing with blocks, simply stacking them in various configurations, and were very competent in this respect. Teachers added natural branches as an option, and a few children arranged branches around their structures. When duct tape and wire were added to the shelving nearby, however, the structures became much more complex in terms of attachment. Lots of experimentation followed: What attaches what in the strongest way? How tall can we go? The more complex materials empowered children to deepen their knowledge of building—and these new materials were always of their own choice to take or leave.

The Role of Loose Parts

The term *loose parts* has become part of the ECE vernacular over the past several years. This term refers to all the wonderful bits and pieces that we might use in our lives (and may then be discarded, even though they are fascinating to children), including natural materials, pieces of machinery, containers, and fasteners of many types. The possibilities are endless; see the list of loose parts within the schema chart in the appendix.

The most important aspect of loose parts is that they provide for all types of play at any level; they act as a catalyst for children's big ideas, and they provide for much practice in "making one thing stand for another," otherwise known as representational or symbolic play.

Let's take a look at some examples of children's work with loose parts:

Fostering Creativity

In any environment, both the degree of inventiveness and creativity, and the possibility of discovery, are directly proportional to the number and kind of variables in it.

—Simon Nicholson

What does this mean for ECE settings? Simply that the more choices of varied and open-ended materials children (and adults!) are exposed to, the more they are likely to come up with inventive and creative ways to use these materials. Time, of course, is of the essence; we need plenty of it in order to be able to fully explore the possibilities of materials.

Children are almost always delighted by having snow brought indoors for exploration. In this case, a further invitation is added through the use of natural materials/loose parts and the challenge of crossing the animals over from one place to another. During this exploration, all types of questions and challenges may arise as the snow melts.

Any exploration of materials can be made richer with the use of mirrors. For example, if children have been working on stacking for some time, looking at their work on top of or in front of mirrors may deepen their inquiry, adding an element of wondering about depth, height, quantity, and distance because the materials will be seen from another perspective.

Shower curtain rings and other circular objects, together with paper towel holders, provide an opportunity for infants to explore loose parts.

Loose parts on a grand scale! In London Bridge's multipurpose room (at the Stoneybrook Early Childhood Learning Centre, in London, Ontario), large loose parts are organized around the large central space. Here is an opportunity for larger inquiries using longer lengths of cardboard, tubing, fabric, and so on. Don't have a multipurpose room? How about taking these types of materials outdoors?

Becoming More Specific as Moments and Interests Evolve

As we observe children of all ages, from infants right through to the early years of formal school, we see that if they are given the opportunity, interesting materials, and the time to play, their ideas often develop into long-term inquiries as they become more and more engaged with the materials and one another. Are you able to recognize when this is happening? How do we know what is actually engaging for the children about this particular material?

Here is an example of how simple play became more complex and then developed into a bigger inquiry:

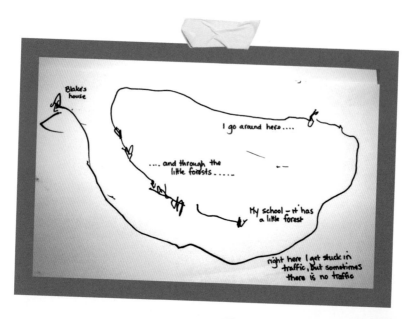

One day, after a group of children discussed how they got to school (by car, walking, bus, and so on) and talked about a long traffic jam, conversations turned to where the children actually lived in the community and what their homes were like. This natural conversation prompted invitations from the teachers to draw how they got to school, to represent their homes, and to build the city in which they live. Different children took up different invitations over time. The inquiry journeyed through a focus on their own homes to their street names, their immediate community, and the larger city. Questions and opinions arose over time; for instance, one child was quite fascinated with apartment buildings and their height and tried to represent this height in many ways. This inquiry proceeded from one focus to another depending upon the children's ideas and tangents.

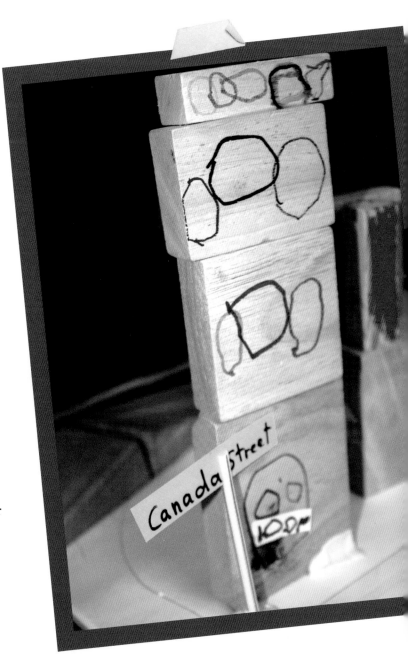

The Curation of Materials: Changing, Responding, and Moving Things Around—Intentional Yet Flexible

As our classroom fills with interesting supplies that children need in order to express ideas, how do we keep all the bits and pieces orderly, accessible to children, and flexible while also being intentional on the teachers' part?

If materials are to be truly accessible, we know they must be both visible and inviting to the children. As teachers, we never have enough storage space and have to become creative and think outside the script as we organize materials. We also have to sometimes let go in terms of our own need for neatness and remember that a beautiful mess is often necessary as children strive to understand the materials or express an idea!

A variety of natural materials are within reach and visible to children, due to open baskets on low shelving. Books that represent and support the children's current inquiry are nearby.

Repurposed furniture, such as this large dresser, provide a space not only for general storage but also for saving and protecting ongoing investigations on slightly higher shelving.

Loose parts of many types are stored together in this kindergarten classroom, ready for work in a nearby open space, along with blocks.

Storage can also be beautiful. In this small studio space, simple jars make tiny objects visible and keep them together while staying accessible to children. Notice that a couple of "inspirations," in the form of art pieces, are also included on this shelving.

The Difference between Invitation and Provocation

The terms *invitation* and *provocation* are sometimes used interchangeably in North America. We also hear the term *proposal* from educators in Reggio Emilia. After many conversations with esteemed colleagues, however, I believe there are subtle differences in the meaning of these words when used in early years settings.

Invitation, for instance, usually refers to materials that are inviting and set up quite loosely for children to respond to or not. Often an invitation can be used to see if an interest that has been observed needs further support or extension, or whether (depending upon the children's responses) it is worth developing into a deeper inquiry.

Provocation, on the other hand, refers to more of a challenge with materials or activities—something that is perhaps unusual, thought provoking, or puzzling and that stimulates a response. This will often be used when children have already shown strong interest in an idea or material; it offers a way to take the investigation further.

Proposal, as used in Reggio Emilia (where the term *provocation* is also widely used), seems to be an exploratory suggestion made by an educator to children, such as, "What if we . . . " or "What, in your opinion, would happen if . . ." This opens a window for children's ideas and thinking to be expressed and supports the teacher in decision making about a further response.

An Environment Full of Provocations and Invitations

One option for supporting children's play explorations and inquiries is to offer an invitation or provocation based on the play we've observed or conversations we've heard during play or routines.

Perhaps you are not sure just yet if this play idea warrants a deeper inquiry. A series of invitations or provocations and the children's responses to them may help you decide how

Not a Stick: After demonstrating engagement with this book, a simple invitation was set up near the block area; this includes the book itself and varied sticks that enable children to explore possibilities.

and when to support a full-scale inquiry for some of the children. (It is rare that a whole group or class of young children will be interested in the same ideas/investigations at the same time, although it does occasionally happen.)

Time and More Time: To Use the Materials, Revisit, Repeat, and Explore

Interesting and engaging materials will attract children; then they need ample time to use them, explore all the possibilities, play out their ideas, and repeat these actions over and over again until they are satisfied and ready to move on.

Given enough time and access, young children will also notice what others are doing with materials. There are several ways they might respond to this noticing:

- They may use the other child's actions as inspiration and try to do something similar.

- They may have an aha moment and think of something different to do with similar materials.

- If verbal, they may ask questions of the other child(ren), their curiosity coming to the forefront, such as, "How did you do that?" or "How did you make that work?"

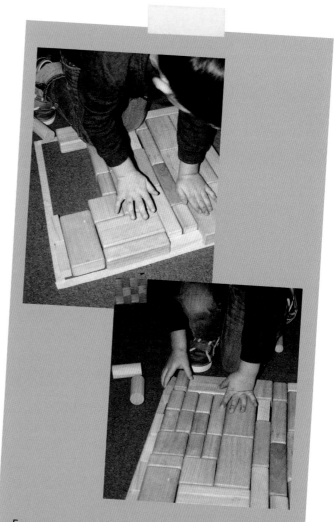

For several weeks at the beginning of the semester in this pre-K classroom, children had been deeply engaged with blocks, figuring out "how they work." Even though some of the children were five years old, they had not previously had much experience with extended block play. In this instance, after watching children line up blocks and piece them together into designs, teachers offered a provocation that involved further challenge: a square of masking tape on the floor. Some children were intrigued with how blocks might fit into this space and experimented with several strategies to discover how this might work. It was puzzling and challenging work that they fully enjoyed, and it led to further competence in the block work that followed.

- They may continue with a previously abandoned investigation after gaining some extra knowledge or new enthusiasm from others.

Throughout this process of children noticing each other's play, it is highly recommended that educators also notice what is going on and document with brief notes or photographs. This is useful data for revisiting with children or thinking through with colleagues.

Giving plenty of time and using flexible time frames means, from the teacher's point of view, not interrupting children who are exploring something that is fascinating to them, even if the schedule says we "should" move on. When thinking about schedules, we are looking at the program through the teacher's lens, not the child's, who has no concept of time. The availability of lengthy time frames for play and flexible schedules (which remain consistent in terms of what happens first, next, and so on) mean that the child has the luxury of time to discover not only what the materials can do but also how the materials can serve the individual child's particular ideas.

The Role of Aesthetics

Beautiful environments invite us in and, in some cases, provoke excitement, inspiration, or even a meditative state. Yet what exactly is beauty in an early childhood environment? Often *beauty* conjures up visions of spaces that are neat and tidy, with wonderful storage and plenty of light. The neatness of a space, however, is again an adult aspiration. While we all strive to be organized in order to have materials easily on hand, the child certainly does not need everything to be worthy of a photo shoot! Instead we might ask ourselves, "What is beautiful to the child?" and, indeed, ask this question of the children themselves. Their responses may be surprising and, at the very least, thought provoking. We can expect different answers from children who live in different countries and cultures and even from different children within the same families!

Here are some children's responses to the question "What makes something beautiful?" At the Cyert Center for Early Education at Carnegie Mellon University, three- and four-year-olds, along with their teachers, examined this question over the long term (Johns and Kemp 2017). This began with the children's idea to make an art gallery on a classroom door, followed by their intention to "create something beautiful and enduring that they could care for in collaboration with the other children" (33). Through conversations, observations, and reflection with children, educators found that "things were determined to be beautiful based on a determination of aesthetics that included form, color, shape, and utility" (38). Children also noted that sounds could be beautiful, as could scents, and over time it became clear to the educators that the children's ideas about beauty were multisensory.

At Madeley Nursery School in the United Kingdom, attention to detail draws our eye upwards. We see interesting materials highlighted by soft lighting.

In this classroom at Madeley, complex materials—including light and shadow—are in close proximity to the children's familiar blocks, creating endless possibilities, as well as being beautiful.

Children and Adults in Relationship with the Environment

What does it mean for humans to be "in relationship" with their environment? When we consider relationships with other people, we may think about relating to them through interactions and actions. Or perhaps we think about an environment where we care for those people in both the practical and emotional sense. As people, we communicate with one another in multiple ways, many of them nonverbal.

The same exact principles apply when we are in relationship with an environment. The environment communicates with us and sends us messages, often inferring a particular mode of action. Also some environments are capable of producing emotions. What kinds of messages or emotions do these environments provoke for you?

When we think about being in relationship with the environment, what does this mean for children? Looking at the following examples, we can consider how these environments may seem friendly to a child, provoke excitement or inspiration, reassure, or challenge:

This arrangement is somewhat provocative. Perhaps the children might wonder how an image carries from the computer screen to the wall or ask themselves, "What are these materials, and what can I do with them?"

Still linked to projection, here is an opportunity for children to wonder, "How can I interact with this image? How can I enter this world?"

These images from Madeley Nursery School demonstrate how children might interact with materials when those materials are complex, interesting, thought provoking, and inviting.

SOMETHING TO TRY . . .

- Take several photographs of your classroom as it usually appears, not staged. Print out a few of them to discuss as a team, paying attention to specific items. Reflect on why that particular piece of equipment is in that particular place and the function it serves. Why, for instance, is the easel placed where it is in the room? Can the children use it independently whenever they want? If not, why not? What function does the easel serve? The whole classroom and its arrangement and function can be examined in this way.

- What message does your classroom send? If you have a tablet or smartphone, use it to pan the room, and then play the video back to reflect on what you see.

- What is the most intriguing material in your classroom for the children? Why is this material so engaging?

- Think about how the children are engaged; are they experimenting, revisiting, and talking?

- How are invitations used in your setting? What is their value?

- How do you and your team think about beauty? What does this mean to you, and how does beauty appear in your classroom?

A "Thinking" Environment That Supports Risk-Taking

There are teaching and learning environments that "play it safe" in terms of how we think about our work and how we approach it, and then there are those that encourage innovation and thinking outside the box for both children and adults.

A play-it-safe environment, for instance, may stay with long-held and traditional approaches, sticking with a script that has worked for them in the past. Other educational settings encourage staff to think critically, examine their work from many perspectives, learn about new approaches in order to consider them (while holding on to their core beliefs and theories), and actively encourage lively discourse where everyone's point of view is heard and carefully considered. When we reflect upon which type of environment might produce innovative and/or inspiring practices or create theory from practice, it is easy to see that the idea of risk taking in our ideas and thinking would be more likely to produce creative ways of being in the classroom. While not advocating change just for the sake of change, a reflective and critical-thinking approach offers possibilities for growth for both teachers and children.

How does a work and play environment go about cultivating such innovative or "risky" thinking, and what does this feel and look like?

Often when we are exposed to new-to-us early years settings in our own country or abroad, we see practices that delight, puzzle, or challenge us. There is huge value in visiting a setting that is completely different from our own, and I would argue that this is one of the most meaningful forms of professional learning for educators. To read about a practice is one thing, but to see that practice in action and to be able to talk about it with educators who are living the practice is another.

Thousands of educators have visited the inspirational schools in Reggio Emilia, Italy. The reasons for joining such study tours are probably as varied as the participants themselves, who come from all over the world to learn more about the approaches used in Reggio schools. They are often intrigued, puzzled, or inspired by the images of values coming to life in practice, decision making that is shared with the children, long-term projects that are awe inspiring in their depth, documentation that is shared with all the protagonists, respect that is given to children's ideas, and environments that support these ideas. The philosophies and beliefs that underlie practices in Reggio Emilia are deep and far reaching—so much so that when unfamiliar with their approaches, it is useful to read important works such as *The Hundred Languages of Children* to understand the history of how their beliefs were put into action.

While the formal lectures within a Reggio study tour are intensely thought provoking, and the physical environments of their schools are sometimes breathtaking, the conversations with the educators themselves or hearing about their inquiry work through presentations is what frequently sparks new thinking—and disequilibrium—for many educators. Some participants, myself included, continue to think about these lectures and reread notes for years after the study tour. They are the source of lively discourse among like-minded people and often help us reconsider our own practices through a different lens. Not everyone can journey to Italy to engage in this type of work, but inquiry-based practice is becoming more and more common and accessible in terms of visiting others' settings in North America, Europe, Australia, New Zealand, and Asia. Wherever you live, you are likely to be able to find local centers or schools that are attempting to apply some aspects of their inspirations from Reggio Emilia. Another useful resource when you are unable to travel even locally is the video *Everyday Utopias*, which enables the viewer to see a "day in the life" of the Diana School in Reggio Emilia, where many of the values of the school become visible through daily routines, encounters with materials, and interactions.

The Role of Disequilibrium

At Pacific Oaks College, where I studied for my master's degree, students were informed from the very beginning of our studies that disequilibrium is a good thing! What did our instructors mean by this, and why did they value disequilibrium—that feeling of discomfort and uncertainty—so much? At that time, Dr. Gretchen Reynolds was teaching for Pacific Oaks. In a 2017 personal communication, she explains that disequilibrium offers the promise of possibility:

> My first teaching position was with first graders in a busy inner-city school in New Jersey. Traditional teaching techniques were the modus operandi in the classroom I inherited and in the first-grade class with whom we shared a coatroom. By the nature of the role and responsibilities expected of the profession, teachers are attributed authority, power, respect, and trust. I was afraid of making a mistake . . . any mistake. After all, I had the reputation of my predecessor to uphold, and my colleague had years of experience to her credit.
>
> The year was fraught with worries, tears, starts and stops, overwork, a "male" guinea pig who gave birth to two pups, and more than one distraught parent. I experimented to make our classroom an interesting place. I deconstructed seating in rows and placed desks in groups of four and six. I offered wonderful poems for reading and writing assignments. Scissors, crayons, paste, and lots of blank sheets of paper replaced a stash of copies of coloring book pages. I made endless trips to the local library for quality children's literature. The classroom was still mayhem from time to time. After all, children and parents were uncertain how to respond when children were asked to choose from a few simple, open-ended activities for part of every day. Things turned around on the Monday I hauled in three large boxes of hardwood blocks (my dad and I had spent a couple of weekends in his basement workshop measuring, sawing, and sanding). They were an invitation to children to build when they had completed "desk work."
>
> My big takeaway from that year was to take risks and to permit myself to learn from children rather than the teachers I thought I should imitate. I made copious notes and watched, observed, and listened to the children when they had opportunities to be self-directed, take initiative, make choices, and play with puzzles, board games, paints, graphic materials, and blocks. Watching and learning from the children, I had no end of

ideas for activities and curriculum that might engage them. I learned that I might not know at the outset what the outcome of an experience would be and that the children's responses would be the gauge of an activity's success.

An understanding of Piaget's theory of cognitive development—and the concept of disequilibrium—was my scaffold. Disequilibrium, as uncomfortable in reality as it may be, can be patiently waited out. Disequilibrium is the edge, the tipping point . . . between assimilation—maintaining the status quo—and accommodation—landing at a new, larger, meaningful place. The visceral response to disequilibrium is discomfort and tension. The promise of disequilibrium is possibility.

Traditional teaching has always been about predictability. Predictability is a polar opposite of disequilibrium. In a classroom, what generates disequilibrium for you? Are open-ended experiences scary? Closed experiences, where learning outcomes are identified (and usually narrow), are safe. Open-ended activities are an opportunity to identify learning outcomes following the activity, not prior to it. A teacher who observes systematically can identify individual children's learning by watching their play and listening to their thinking while they work with open-ended materials, explore the woods, discuss rules for outside play, and interact with friends.

Vivian Gussin Paley, known for her writing about preschool and kindergarten teaching at the University of Chicago lab schools, maintains that disequilibrium in the company of children is teaching effectiveness. One of Vivian's stories is of a question she asked children about peanut butter and jelly sandwiches: what do we have more of—peanut butter and jelly sandwiches or jelly sandwiches? Quite simply, they did not get it. They stared at her blankly. "Confusion—mine or theirs—is as natural a condition as clarity. The natural response to confusion is to keep trying to connect what you already know to what you don't know. . . . We must listen with curiosity and great care to the main characters who are, of course, the children" (1986, 131).

Outside of college, what effect does disequilibrium have on our daily lives with children? Within inquiry-based, emergent settings, one of the most important feelings to accept is that of uncertainty. What might you be uncertain about? Educators who have embraced inquiry with young children have told me about some of their initial struggles:

- *How do I make a decision about which line of inquiry/interest to follow?* There will be many ideas from children that crop up at the same time! Trust your judgment on this. Do children show deep engagement with an idea, excitement, or industry with materials? If you're unsure about making this decision, try offering an invitation to find out more. Talk with your colleagues about what they have noticed and their interpretations.

- *What if only two or three children are engaged in this investigation?* This is fine. We tend to work in teams, and once the materials are provided, we can split the work of following more than one inquiry at the same time, observing from time to time and provisioning the environment in response to what happens next.

- *What kinds of materials should I provide?* This is where the magic of loose parts comes to the forefront. Open-ended materials can "be" anything that the child requires them to be, without huge expenditures for the classroom. Also, know that children often come up with very unusual topics of investigation. In my own experience, these topics have included holes, chocolate, quilts, and cleaning polluted water. The only materials we were able to provide for these investigations were not purchased but found, and the children were easily able to make use of them.

Uncertainty may cause discomfort for some educators. When we are observing children and then reflecting to find the meaning in their actions, we can never be 100 percent sure that we are correct. And this is just fine. We can accept our uncertainty and its accompanying discomfort, use it to create questions, and then try to explore those questions with the children, collaborating and co-constructing as we move together on our journey of learning.

When working in an inquiry-based setting that uses play as a foundation, over time we can expect to become more at ease with disequilibrium. In fact, most educators who work in this way find it extremely exciting. When children say or do or ask about something unexpected, we become somewhat like detectives, figuring out how to find answers, how to support children, what else to pay attention to, and so on. It adds a liveliness to our work, because we—along with the children—are wondering. This wonder keeps the passion in our work.

While it is sometimes a new teaching approach or vein of thinking that causes disequilibrium for educators, at other times the children's questions or topics of investigation may make us feel uncomfortable and question the wisdom of following this line of inquiry with them. (See chapter 8 for an extended example of risky topics and inquiry.)

Children Using Materials in New or "Risky" Ways

Sometimes children use materials in ways that feel uncomfortable for teachers. While one of our important roles is to protect the children's safety—both physical and psychological—there are times when we seem to prevent them from using materials in unfamiliar ways simply because these ways are unusual for us. This is where we must pause to reflect. What exactly is discomfiting about this? What are our own past experiences that may lead to this discomfort? Have we ourselves ever tried what the children are doing? What is our own tolerance for experimentation with materials? Most important, can we see the value or learning that may occur from using the materials in this way? What are the possibilities?

Let's consider some examples of usual ways to use materials:

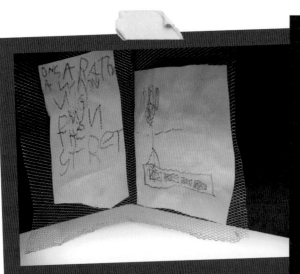

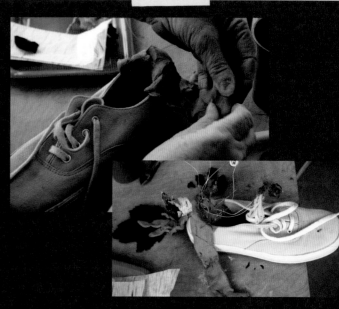

When children began sculpting in many different ways in the studio area, they were offered flexible mesh as an option. We thought that perhaps they would learn that mesh could be a support for a malleable material such as clay. To our surprise, one child (after much messing about!) discovered instead that mesh can be folded in two. This led him to think about books, and, as a result, he produced his own story and illustration. While this was a completely different result from what the teachers intended, it was nonetheless valuable, intriguing, and something that we could follow up on with questions such as, "What makes a book?"

When teachers are given similar opportunities to explore unusual or new-to-them materials, much learning takes place, and our discomfort with using things in unusual ways may wane. Here an educator in a workshop on loose parts and the role of materials in the environment investigates the combination of an old sneaker and clay. What are the possibilities, and what was she thinking about? Reflecting on these questions during such a workshop helped us reflect more deeply on the unusual things that children may do.

Into the Forest We Go—Inquiry and Risk Outdoors

As forest schools, sometimes referred to as nature schools or outdoor classrooms, become more a part of our early childhood practice, we have an opportunity to encompass all that we believe about children's and teachers' thinking, environments, inquiry, and risk—and to take our innovative thinking outdoors with us.

Whatever we call these outdoor environments and the curricula or approaches that may unfold there, these early childhood programs have some common characteristics:

- Generally, the majority of the day—or at least a good part of it—is spent outdoors in a natural space; this space, whether a field or forest or farm, is recognized and valued as an important learning environment, usually the *main* learning environment for their program. Weather is not considered a daunting challenge unless the windchill is dangerous. Families know that the children will be outdoors and dress them for it. In some centers (such as ForestKids in Nova Scotia, Canada), outdoor gear is provided, and nature provides the materials to investigate.

- For many centers around the world, such spaces do not exist nearby, so educators have adapted "traditional" playgrounds to more natural ones that do not consist of commercial equipment but rather grassed areas with berms and tunnels, tree trunks, and many loose parts. Not only are these less expensive to develop than, let's say, a massive climbing frame, but they also offer more opportunities—many of them novel to the children—for inquiry and adventurous play, such as balancing on a long wobbly branch that is sitting on the ground, discovering insects underneath it, finding water in unusual places and wondering how it got there, and so on.

- Inquiry in such spaces develops naturally. According to Claire Warden, a long-time advocate of and practitioner in Nature Kindergartens and Forest Schools in Scotland, "affordances are highly dynamic, with different features, elements and materials affording different play experiences for different individuals on different occasions. Every day is different; the moisture, temperature, light, movement in natural spaces is changing constantly, stimulating new ideas and perspectives" (2012, 71).

What Are Affordances?

Affordances, as defined by Warden, are "opportunities that arise from the interaction between the physical properties of the environment and the interests, ideas and intent of the individual. Affordances arise through active detection: where the person is sensing and moving, observing and acting at the same time" (2012, 70).

In some countries, forest schools are nothing new; they have long been embedded in cultures as a whole, in early years settings in particular. Such is the case in Denmark, and we can learn much about inquiry outdoors, and management of risk, from their practices.

Jane Williams-Siegfredsen (2017, 65) outlines the Danish early years curriculum in her book *Understanding the Danish Forest School Approach*:

The curriculum for early years settings in Denmark became law in 2004 and every institution has to make an institutional curriculum plan that covers six areas of learning:

1. The child's all-around personal development

2. Social development

3. Language

4. Body and movement

5. Nature and natural phenomenon

6. Cultural expression and values

Within these six areas, the pedagogues should facilitate four learning processes: "to be able," "to experience," "to enjoy," and "to understand."

We can see from this outline, although by no means a comprehensive view of the Danish curriculum, that there is space here for inquiry, understanding through experience, and, most important, enjoying these processes.

How does the process of inquiry unfold outdoors in a Danish nature kindergarten? Children out in the forest every day notice changes in this familiar environment, some seasonal, some natural, and some made by humans; all are ripe for investigation by the children. The teachers' role in these schools, as in most schools that support inquiry, is to listen, prompt, and support. Children construct their own knowledge of this outdoor world over time, and, of course, questions develop. Sometimes these come from natural curiosity and wonder, sometimes from misunderstandings, and sometimes from a true puzzle, such as when the children found a snake skin. A child asked, "How can the snake live without its skin?" which, of course, offered up the chance for teachers and children to investigate this phenomenon further, together, as collaborators (Williams-Siegfredsen 2017).

A North American Example of an Outdoor Environment: Small World Learning Centre, Bridgewater

The philosophy held at Small World Learning Centre in Bridgewater, Nova Scotia, is one in which the outdoors is simply treated as another play and learning space. Inspired by the practices of Reggio Emilia, the center chooses many indoor materials that reflect the outdoors and the community, and the outdoors is used constantly throughout the whole year in rain, shine, or snow.

Within the trees, children have a wide array of loose parts, including tires and an old pallet, with which to work. Here they are fashioned by the children into a temporary seating space.

Forest surrounds this child care center, and the children use this land for exploring and fort building. Following are some images of the types of work and play that the children regularly engage in outdoors:

Within the fence, sensory experiences and dramatic play are heightened by the inclusion of a mud kitchen. Inquiries can easily take place here as the materials change according to the children's ideas.

We know that young children love enclosures, and building and being inside enclosures can become a schema. This one was literally grown from seed and provides solitude, shade, or a cozy space for two or three.

Art can happen anywhere, and here the "easels" are affixed to trees. Such inspiration can be found outdoors for painting, drawing, and modeling. The light is dappled, and that factors into the children's art as they either work with shadows or around them.

Other seating is provided in several sizes, constructed easily by a parent with a chainsaw. The many heights of chairs mean that even the youngest students can use them.

Do you limit the length of branches and sticks that children can use? Do you allow them to be used at all? Sometimes, educators worry about the physical risk of using branches. Yet in those settings that use them, provided the children know how to handle them and assuming that supervision is nearby, the possibilities for their use are endless. Here children are partway through constructing a habitat using long pole-like branches that they have found within the forest and toted to where they are needed. These are engaging and memorable structures for the children, and it is likely that many educators remember this type of work from their own childhood.

At ForestKids in Hammonds Plains, Nova Scotia, children also spend much of their days, sometimes including mealtimes and naps, in the forest. This child care center understands the challenges for families of dressing their child for whatever weather the day may bring in this unpredictable coastal climate, so it provides rain suits, bright vests, and brimmed sun hats. Assembling this system has taken some years but has been worth the effort, as every child is equipped for all kinds of weather and playful inquiry.

The idea of risk taking is often attached to the outdoors, even though risk can and does occur anywhere and everywhere; it is simply a part of life. Some educators may feel that they have less control in a large, natural space. Or perhaps the element of the unknown is unsettling. In an era where obesity is common and physical activity is on the decline for both adults and children, however, we owe it to children to closely examine our own feelings about the outdoors, learn more (through reading, seminars, and simply "getting out there"), and take some steps to at least try out some simple outdoor inquiries. You won't have to observe for long to understand that children are in their element when outside, and, over time, we can all learn how to make this a safe and regular part of their lives.

Here I will return to Warden, who echoes my own thoughts on risk so succinctly:

> Adults should not make a judgment about the hazards that may lead to a risk, without at the same time making a judgment about what benefits it might bring to children. For all the activities that children need and want to undertake in our settings, we do a benefit-risk analysis where we do a comparison of the risk of a situation to its related benefits. (2012, 109)

Of course we want to keep children safe. We also want them to have optimal opportunities to explore, inquire, and learn. We must remember that we are in relationship with these children; they are not strangers to us. Therefore we recognize their particular capabilities, competencies, and judgment. For instance, it comes somewhat naturally to small children—if we allow climbing to happen—for them to stop when they feel unsafe. We can actually pose the question "Does that feel safe?" and if the answer is no, there is a learning opportunity. How do you safely descend from a height that does not feel safe? How do we scaffold this? Better that children learn to handle some of the risks that naturally occur in life than to proceed unprepared. We protect them, yes, and we also help them to learn their way through situations to gain confidence and to be prepared.

Whether indoors or outside, it is the flexibility of the teachers' responses to children's actions, their welcoming of different points of view and perspectives, and their knowledge of multiple philosophies and approaches to learning that empower children to forge ahead with their inquiries in innovative ways. We do, however, have to find ways to help make these inquiries happen.

Finding Ways to Say Yes

Laurel Fynes is an experienced kindergarten teacher in Ontario, Canada, who has been working with inquiry-based and emergent curricula for some time. Here are her thoughts on learning to "say yes" to her children's ideas:

> I am already consciously making an effort to say "yes" to students when years ago I would have said "No"; "No" to climbing a fence, building structures above my head, using scissors for materials thicker than cardboard, pouring water away from the safe confines of the water table, using loose parts and playdough away from their original center. I'm not saying I always say yes, but I use my knowledge of the context (the student, the material, the situation) as my guide, and try to remember that there is always a lesson to be learned from taking a negotiated risk. Sometimes I don't say yes or no, but turn the question back to the students. (2014)

Laurel makes an important point: when in relationship with children, and when we are respectful of their capabilities, we know when it is safe to say yes, even if the idea is unconventional in our setting or might appear somewhat risky. It is the relationship—not only rules that are "written in stone"—that is the basis for decision making. While we must adhere to regulations for our settings, there is usually some room for flexibility. Laurel goes on:

> A big idea I hope to impart (whether to parents, special guests, or valuable long-term additions like ECE or teacher candidates) is that the direction of the learning is always negotiated with the learners in the room. This means continually changing plans, adapting centers or materials to support new directions, and letting go of ideas we adults have when the students come up with better ones. It is the change in my own teaching practice that has had more impact than any other, including removing "must-do" activities from our daily schedule, relaxing rules about how many may use a center, area, or toy, indeed even how furniture is used. Another way to say it: I have actively tried to stop saying "no" to ideas, even those that sound implausible. Once students know the basic rules of the room (we expect respect for learners and learning environment) they are able to make many choices each day (during our "play and learn time") without hearing the words "no" or "stop."
>
> . . . This is what is wonderful in a classroom of engaged learners: once students follow their interests and have developed the social and emotional skills to direct their learning, I am able to flit from area to area or sit down and join in the fun. (2014)

Laurel's practice of and belief in knowing the children well, understanding their social skills, and creating some manageable expectations for respect all contribute to children being able to direct their own play and inquiries, empowering them to make safe and reasonable decisions. And usually in a richly provisioned environment where children also contribute to its maintenance, the teachers are able to sit back at some points during play to observe, listen, and take notes that will inform their future teaching decisions.

It is not only the children who benefit from flexibility and innovative thinking that may seem out of the ordinary or feel risky. Teachers themselves benefit from allowing their own curiosity to flourish within the classroom. Why is curiosity an important trait in an educator? Let's explore this in chapter 4 as we examine environments that encourage curiosity and questioning.

SOMETHING TO TRY . . .

- Reflect upon the idea of risky thinking. Are you able to step out of conventions and think about routines, curricula, and environments in ways that are new to you? If not, what gets in the way? What small steps or experiments could you attempt to help you explore new-to-you approaches?

- Critical thinking involves reflection on aspects of our teaching and learning. Take one part of your day (for example, meeting time) and think it through. Why is it there? What are your intentions? What works and what does not?

- At your next staff or team meeting, experiment with the materials yourselves, perhaps using them in unusual combinations. How might you use wire, leaves, and clay together, for instance? What about water, mirrors, and stones? Afterward, discuss the new or unusual possibilities that opened up for you. How might this affect your teaching practice?

- Examine how you use your outdoor space. Go outside and ignore the equipment that is already there. If it were taken away, what else exists? What could you do with the natural environment that remains? What might the children discover?

An Environment That Promotes Curiosity and Questioning—For Both Children and Teachers

> "For everyone involved, the real connection is questions."

This quote from a conversation with teachers and the pedagogista at Iqbal Misbah school in Reggio Emilia, Italy, during a Canadian study tour in 2015 resonated deeply for me. I wondered how many of us spend our days in early childhood settings trying to *answer* questions about children and their actions instead of also *asking* them of ourselves! How would our days change if we practiced in a culture of questioning originating in our genuine curiosity about what children are doing and saying?

My guess is that this perspective might be very new as well as eye opening for some educators. Indeed, in my work with both student teachers and seasoned practitioners, I often see educators struggle to formulate questions about what children are doing. How can we cultivate a stance of curiosity about what children are doing and what their actions mean? Why is curiosity important as a teacher disposition? How does curiosity support an inquiry-based curriculum? In this chapter, we will hear from educators and directors who recognize children's natural curiosity and act upon it but equally value teachers' curiosity and take steps to nurture it.

First, what exactly do we mean by curiosity? How would you define it? Eugene Cernan, a US astronaut, describes the term in this way:

> Curiosity is the essence of human existence. Who are we? Where are we? Where are we going? I don't know. I don't have any answers to those questions. I don't know what's over there around the corner. But I want to find out.

Curiosity, then, might be defined as the desire to learn and know about anything, and children—as well as many adults—are full of curiosity.

Curiosity in Children

We think of children as being naturally curious, and indeed they are from birth. They enter the world wide eyed, curious to know what's over the fence or around the corner or under a rock. They simply have to find out. As soon as they are able to move, they are on a quest to learn more about the world.

We have seen in previous chapters how a rich environment full of engaging and open-ended materials can promote and support curiosity and, therefore, inquiry. How, though, can teachers' own actions and dispositions encourage curiosity in children? At London Bridge Child Care Services in London, Ontario, leaders have given a great deal of thought to this disposition. Here are their thoughts about the importance of curiosity within their organization:

> At London Bridge Child Care Services our mission statement reads *"We nurture curious minds and kind hearts."*
>
> These are things we've come to understand about environments that nurture curiosity:

Embrace the Unknown

Asking questions where the answers are not known creates lively discussions and opens a space for the sharing of many perspectives. Lingering in the unknown creates a desire to learn more and there is an excitement when we make discoveries with others. By not knowing we are pushed beyond our own thinking and we consider what we can learn from theory, research, and best practice. Without curiosity, we are destined to a prescribed outcome.

Relationships Are Key

Relationships are at the heart of everything that we do. When we nurture relationships we automatically nurture curiosity. It is through our curiosity that we begin to know and understand others better; who they are and what they think. Being curious about each other helps us avoid making assumptions and jumping to judgment. It opens dialogue while navigating conflict and focuses on finding the best solutions. There is an aspect of vulnerability as we dig into values and biases and we need to be kind to ourselves as we learn and grow.

Know Yourself

This requires us to be researchers of ourselves and ask questions that can help us understand our impact and evolve our practices. It is about developing an understanding of who we really are; our likes, dislikes, and our thinking. We learn about the moments that capture our attention. By questioning our certainties we expand our view of our role as Educators. It is important to develop the habit of self-reflection by making time every day to think about our own thinking.

Be Intentional

Intentionality is about knowing what we want and taking deliberate steps to get there. By carving out time to come together (team meetings, Communities of Practice and professional learning) we support dialogue across our organization. Thinking protocols like *The Thinking Lens* helps us reflect on and guide our responses in the classroom. This intentional way of being pushes thinking and grows our practice.

Evolve Regularly

As we encounter new ideas and thinking our understandings grow. Our work is fluid. It requires us to be open to the evolution of our habits. By giving ourselves permission to let go of current thoughts, we learn to embrace change and rethink the status quo.

Learn from Children

Children are born with an innate sense of curiosity and have brains that are built for learning. Their interest in the world is inspiring and we look to them as our teachers. They do not have preconceived ideas about how things are done and so they question everything. They teach us to think outside of the box about how and why we do things. We are fortunate to be surrounded by our youngest citizens who remind us to be curious every day.

This mission statement and the ensuing points that further explain how London Bridge's modus operandi is put into action are impressive in that they address *a way of being* rather than what educators within this organization should be "striving to achieve." We know that when adults are supported in being and acting in a certain way within their work environment, hard-and-fast "rules" for what unfolds in the classroom are not needed. Rather the excitement of shared curiosity about what children are doing and why they are doing things in this way drives creative thinking and a rich and responsive curriculum. While standards exist in all licensed child care centers and schools and must be met, these standards can be met through inquiry. The recognition—the noticing—of how we are meeting these standards is an important part of inquiry that can be learned. Many ECE training facilities spend time on this "noticing and recognizing" of what is going on, and in North America, much professional learning is focused on this aspect.

One or two things especially speak to me from London Bridge's way of being:

- "It is through our curiosity that we begin to know and understand others better; who they are and what they think. Being curious about each other helps us avoid making assumptions and jumping to judgment. It opens dialogue while navigating conflict and focuses on finding the best solutions. There is an aspect of vulnerability as we dig into values and biases and we need to be kind to ourselves as we learn and grow." This stance of curiosity about one another as educators—who we are and what we stand for—can only lead to greater understanding of how we respond and make decisions. This is important during inquiries by children, when teachers often have to make decisions while not being entirely sure of where this may lead or if they are on track with the children's thinking. There may be curiosities from teachers about different aspects of the children's work or what they have said. Therefore it is critically important to have a trusting and authentic relationship with our coworkers that empowers us to engage in deep and lively discussions. We do not have to agree, but we do have to engage, listen, respect others' viewpoints, and be able to express our own. This type of relationship grows from deep trust.

- "Without curiosity, we are destined to a prescribed outcome." A prescribed outcome, of course, is exactly what we don't want in an emergent, inquiry-based practice. Instead we are searching for insights from the children themselves, which will lead us to further learning for all the protagonists in the classroom.

If we want children to follow their natural curiosity about how the world works, then we must model this attitude.

- If we want children to be inquirers, to ask questions and explore as a way of learning, we must model this way of being in the world.

- As children play and investigate, we are co-constructors of learning alongside them; therefore we must be genuinely curious.

- As we observe children at play working with materials, we must allow ourselves to wonder and to be open to possibilities.

Developing Inquiry-Based Curriculum from Ideas, Questions, and Curiosity

If we hold an image of children and teachers as inquirers and use this image to develop curriculum, the result will be a practice that is collaborative, engaging for all protagonists, thought provoking, and meaningful.

Rather than following a script for action or relying on developmental goals, we can choose instead to create an environment where children's questions and ideas are valued, where teachers think deeply and respond to these ideas, and where there is permission—for teachers as well as children—to break away from the usual scripts and dare to explore unusual topics or investigate in unusual ways.

At first this may feel a little uncomfortable for some. In an inquiry-based environment, curriculum is often emergent, which means that educators may not always be sure about what will happen next. This does not mean that it is unintentional. Rather, it is a case of slowing down. Educators will have to wait to see what their invitations and observations tell them and then respond. It is reassuring, however, to see how quickly young children become engaged, and it is not hard to understand why. When their ideas and questions are used as a basis for next steps, their play and ideas are valued and sustained.

Why Do We Do What We Do?

When we hold our image of the child as a central focus (what you believe about children, their capabilities, and way of being in the world), we can then think about how our values surrounding children and childhood might become visible in the classroom. Within reflective practice—reflecting on our actions and reactions to children—there is an opportunity to put our values about children and teaching at the forefront.

When we regularly examine long-held scripts, asking the question "Why?" about every part of our daily practices and routines, we are making space for our values to bubble to the surface. Do we really believe, for instance, that young children need to learn how to sit still and pay attention to the teacher? Do we value that practice? Or do we value putting the children's energy, both mental and physical, to better use? If we value the latter, how does that look in our meeting/circle times? Perhaps this value might be made visible through action with materials, the sharing of children's ideas (orally or through documentation), physical action as a mode of learning, and so on.

If an adult newcomer entered your classroom, what values would be visible to that person? How is children's thinking made visible? How are their cultures valued? What can we say about the teaching teams' values as we look around the classroom? If our aim is to be true to the values we hold, we can be intentional about how these values appear, both physically in our classrooms and also in our daily practices. Sometimes these values are shared—such as when stated in a mission or vision statement for an organization—and sometimes they are personally held values that simply matter deeply to us. Either way, they are important to acknowledge, reflect upon, discuss with our teaching team or partner, and bring forward through our actions.

Other than invitations, observations, and responses, how else might we begin to think about our planning process and our intentions? Recently I have been engaged in a great deal of collaboration with educators around the idea of using their values (that is, their image of the child and their role as a teacher in response to this image) as an alternate way of thinking about curriculum. For instance, if we imagine that you value relationships, curiosity, and children's thinking within your day-to-day practice, keeping these values in mind will have a profound effect on how you develop curriculum.

For the educator, there is a shift here. Rather than providing "something to do" or planning in response to a framework or set of prescribed outcomes, an inquiry-based environment can truly center on the child and the values you hold about children, teaching, and learning.

For a reflective practitioner, the learning outcomes will be there; we simply have to recognize them.

This beloved book had been read many, many times in our classroom. Children understood the humor in the book, as well as Harry's "trickiness" throughout the story. They enjoyed the fact that he was also a little naughty! As an invitation, teachers provided both black and white paper at the easel; we wondered how they would represent this story, if at all. Some children did, and it was interesting to see how they strategized when trying to paint a white dog with black spots, or a black dog with white spots, on black or white backgrounds. There is a lot of learning going on here. Can you identify the book?

After exploring rulers for some weeks during play in the block area, children spontaneously began using them for other purposes. For instance, here a ruler is used as a base for lining up pencils that have been sharpened to different lengths. This is not an activity that was set up by the teacher in order to assess children's learning about height; this simply occurred during play because the materials were nearby and the children had the freedom to use them in different areas of the room. However, from viewing what happened, we can see that this child knows about putting things in order according to height. If you are required to assess this skill, this is useful information. In addition, this child can think divergently, independently using materials in varied ways.

Responding to Children's Questions and Statements: How Do We See and "Hear" Children?

Environments that support inquiry need to have systems for observing, reflecting, and responding that are usable for educators. They must work at a practical, everyday level so that educators have both the time and the motivation to use them.

For instance, when do we observe and what types of moments are we watching for? What kinds of things are we listening for?

Finding time to observe is surely the biggest obstacle for most educators. We are not talking about "standing back to watch," however. Few of us have that luxury. Instead we are immersed in our work with children—doing whatever needs to be done at the time in the practical and supportive sense—while simultaneously practicing a habit of *noticing*. How are children using materials? Responding to our invitations? What are they saying as they play—to one another or to us? What strikes us as important, puzzling, interesting, or thought provoking? We need to hold on to these aspects until we can think more deeply about them. Photography is an incredibly helpful tool in this respect, since photographs can "hold in mind" those fleeting moments that we don't have time to write about or think about on the spot. However, it is important to return to them as soon as possible, before the question or thought you had in mind disappears!

This process is a cycle of inquiry and, if used consistently, can become a habit of being in the classroom. There are many graphic representations of this cycle (see Chapter 1), but it always involves observing children carefully, reflecting on what we've seen, documenting as we go, making decisions based on this observation and reflection, and then responding and observing again. Curriculum is developed day by day, with play continuing all around us—perhaps some small project work, perhaps some long-term endeavors—all of it meaningful to the children and exciting to us educators as we see the depth developing in children's strategies and thinking.

Here is an example of children's struggles and teachers' wonderings and questions as they investigate how to make dirty water clean again, an investigation that began with simple water play and an important element of curiosity from children: what happens to dirty water from the toilet?

Most children are quite fascinated to watch as water disappears in a swirl down the toilet bowl. These particular children watched this process over and over again but also asked, "How does the dirty water get clean again?" Although the adults in the room knew a little about this process, we did need to do some research of our own in order to think about next steps.

Cleaning Our Water: An Ecological Project Emerging from Children's Curiosity

The initial questions from the children demonstrated their curiosity in everyday, seemingly (at least to adults!) mundane events. From listening to children's conversations, however, we understood that they had never seen the inside of a toilet tank, so the first thing that teachers did was remove the lid so the children could see the toilet's inner workings.

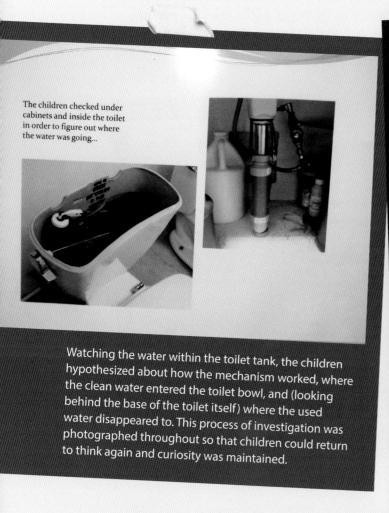

The children checked under cabinets and inside the toilet in order to figure out where the water was going...

Watching the water within the toilet tank, the children hypothesized about how the mechanism worked, where the clean water entered the toilet bowl, and (looking behind the base of the toilet itself) where the used water disappeared to. This process of investigation was photographed throughout so that children could return to think again and curiosity was maintained.

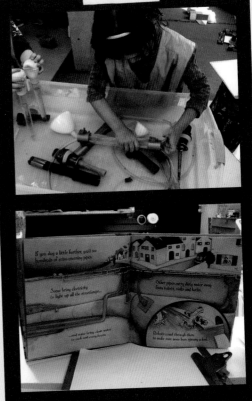

Water play had always been popular in this room, and at this time, some leftover plumbing supplies from a teacher's home were added to the water. Accompanied by an age-appropriate nonfiction book, more information was gathered through play, messing about with pipes, and looking at illustrations. This type of play continued for several days.

As we watched and listened to the children over the next couple of weeks, we ourselves were curious about the children's prior knowledge. A new sewage treatment plant had been in the news in our city—television and newspapers were full of reports about the brand-new system breaking down. We were curious if the children had heard about this and, if so, what their level of understanding was.

Further conversations and sharing of documentation with families uncovered that several families had been talking about the local news, and indeed the children had some prior knowledge of "how toilet water is cleaned." This is where another question arose for teachers: could children draw their theories of what happened to the water as it made its way to the nearby ocean? The invitation was made to children, and several responded with drawings.

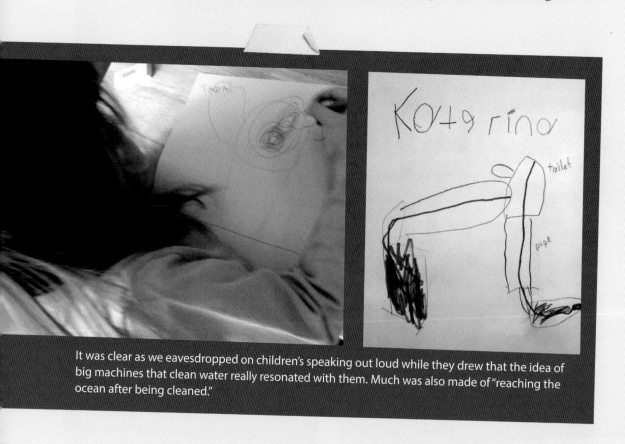

It was clear as we eavesdropped on children's speaking out loud while they drew that the idea of big machines that clean water really resonated with them. Much was also made of "reaching the ocean after being cleaned."

What followed, over several weeks, were many experiments with child-invented filters, including gravel, sand, and coffee filters as they remembered what their family members used at home.

We can see from this initial question about something as ordinary as a toilet that inquiries can emerge from anywhere. It is important not to wait for only "big ideas" to emerge from major play events and philosophical conversations, but also to pay attention to the everyday smaller questions that arise . . . even in the bathroom!

Drawing Out Teachers' Questions

What kind of teaching and learning environment pays attention to teachers' questions and values them? Rather than putting these puzzles or "cognitive knots" on the back burner, we must find ways to record them in order to reflect when the time arises. Some teachers use a simple log book, jotting down their thoughts and questions throughout the day. Others use adhesive notes and find a particular place to collect them. One of the most exciting ways to collect our thoughts, however, is to keep a kind of "sketch-and-word" diary that combines thumbnail photos, quick notes, sketches, and so on—anything that will hold our thinking in mind while we reflect and make decisions. Here is an example from Madeley Nursery School in the United Kingdom:

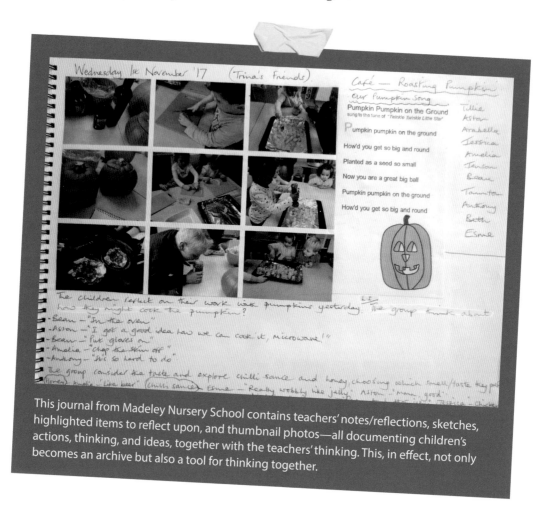

This journal from Madeley Nursery School contains teachers' notes/reflections, sketches, highlighted items to reflect upon, and thumbnail photos—all documenting children's actions, thinking, and ideas, together with the teachers' thinking. This, in effect, not only becomes an archive but also a tool for thinking together.

Besides being a record of what actually happened and a beginning point for developing curriculum, this type of diary can also become a valuable archive: How did we begin this inquiry? Where did it go? How did we make our decisions? It is a tremendously valuable tool for reflection and a long-term record of our journeys with children.

As we examine these types of teacher records, we often recognize repeated patterns in children's play and ideas (schemas), aha moments that occur for teachers, and, of course, things that provoke teacher curiosity and questions.

What kinds of questions are we referring to? Often "developmental" questions are the ones that arise first, almost as a kind of default setting. For example, in the following photograph that involves making a map, we might ask a question about what this child knows about spatial relationships or literacy. And this is a valid stance if you are thinking only about assessment.

However, we could create an entirely different kind of question if we use a wider lens. We might instead wonder how children make sense of their world through symbolic language. This is a question that is broad in scope and offers up much for discussion, and it has implications for classroom practices. For instance, if, after reflection and discussion, we decide that there are many "languages" through which children express their knowledge about the world at large, then our actual classroom, as well as the opportunities within it, may need to be adjusted in order to provide these languages.

Perhaps our bigger questions may be very difficult to answer, and we become "stuck." Rather than treating this situation as a problem, we can embrace it as an opportunity to research the answer within our classroom, trying different approaches, materials, and invitations until we feel we have learned more. We slow down a little and take time to think, giving ourselves permission not to know all the answers immediately.

For instance, during the Movie Project at Halifax Grammar School in Halifax, Nova Scotia, the children had

What Are Schema?

When you are working closely with and carefully observing young children, you will often notice big and small play ideas that they repeat over and over again. These play ideas—burying items, transporting things around the room, jumping off various surfaces, creating patterns, and so on—seem to be completely absorbing for the child. We might wonder, "What is this child attempting to do or to find out?" and "Why is this so absorbing?"

Piaget first used the term *schema* to describe a way of organizing information and understanding something within our world. These days educators use this term to refer to "a repeated pattern of behavior a child employs in order to explore and learn about his or her environment. . . . A child may exhibit an interest in one dominant schema or many schemas at the same time. One schema may be connected with another" (Thornhill 2015, 6).

When we are a little puzzled about what a child is doing and why, we can use the language of schemas to describe what we are seeing, leading to further understanding on the part of the teacher and the ability to support the child further. In this way, we can view schemas as simply another tool in our toolbox of reflecting and understanding.

Here are some schema that you may recognize in the play of young children: Connecting, Trajectory, Enclosing/Enveloping, Dynamic Vertical, Rotation, Going through a Barrier, Transporting, Ordering/Positioning, Transformation, Dynamic Horizontal, and Orientation/Perspective (Stacey 2018).

great difficulty figuring out how to make their "movies" (several 2-D drawings) actually move. It was also very difficult for teachers to devise questions or invitations/materials that would provoke the construction of knowledge without handing information to the children. During an inquiry, after all, we aim for children to construct knowledge and enjoy the process of discovery and learning how to learn. So the question arises: how might materials provide a pathway for discovery?

Since we had frequently recognized that the children had a "sense of story" (that is, a beginning, middle, and end) and since they were capable of putting their story pictures in order, I wondered which materials we had on hand might offer a way to give a sense of movement.

The Hundred Languages of Children

Loris Malaguzzi often referred to the way that children use action and materials (graphics, dance, sculpting, and so on) to express what they know of the world—their expertise expressed in various forms. We can never be absolutely sure of someone else's thinking, but we can further consider the word *language* in order to delve deeper. In a recent meeting with our Emergent Curriculum Community of Practice, for instance, Dr. Carol Anne Wien asked the provocative question, "What do we mean by *language*?" and as you might expect, a huge and deep discussion followed. What has to be there in order for something to be a language? Perhaps, we thought, it is the intent to express an idea, to create meaning, or to refer to something intentional.

Making Movies with Frames

The children—during another project about photography—had experimented with frames, holding them up to various objects around the room to frame them. I offered frames again, not sure of how these might help, and the children at first used them to frame each illustration.

But then they quickly changed their idea, sliding the frames along their illustration/stories to gain a sense of movement. This was exciting for me to see, because when I first asked myself this question about materials, I was unsure of the answer. It was the children and their experimentation that provided me with insight about the power of materials during inquiry.

Yet the drawings/movie illustrations were still not moving. Even so, movie play continued, with the lining up of chairs, selling of tickets, and so on. I noticed that one or two children in particular were concerned with this idea of movement. Thinking back once more, teachers remembered the use of projection on our old overhead projector, which was a staple piece of equipment in the classroom. The children did not seem to remember the role of projection in displaying items on a wall. After a morning meeting thinking together about how to get pictures moving, we asked once more about the children's previous experiences at movie theaters. Finally, a child remembered that "a light comes out of the wall," and we were on our way forward again. Some simple invitations of acetate and markers, together with some objects to represent a favorite story, were placed near the projector. We did not know how the children would react to these but were simply curious as to what might happen.

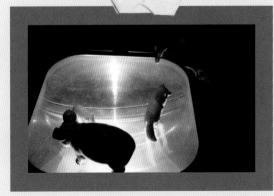

The children used these props to take their play one step further. But then, as often happens, the unexpected occurred. A child who had previous knowledge of how flip-books work suddenly made a little book of his own, took it behind one of our sheet/screens, and flipped through his illustration, resulting in a rudimentary form of movement!

Great excitement followed from the other children and from teachers, and this event reminded us of the power of prior knowledge and what it can bring to an inquiry as children make connections.

Using their knowledge of stories, particularly fairy tales, we continued to explore all the ways to tell a story with movement, and a different child brought up the idea of puppets. Almost immediately another child remembered shadow puppets, which they had made before. A frantic surge of energy—gathering materials, finding a flashlight, using our homemade screen—resulted (days afterward) in an image that was visible and movable. This was satisfying to the children, and they almost immediately moved on to another investigation.

The teachers' curiosities remained long after the children had finished solving this cognitive knot.

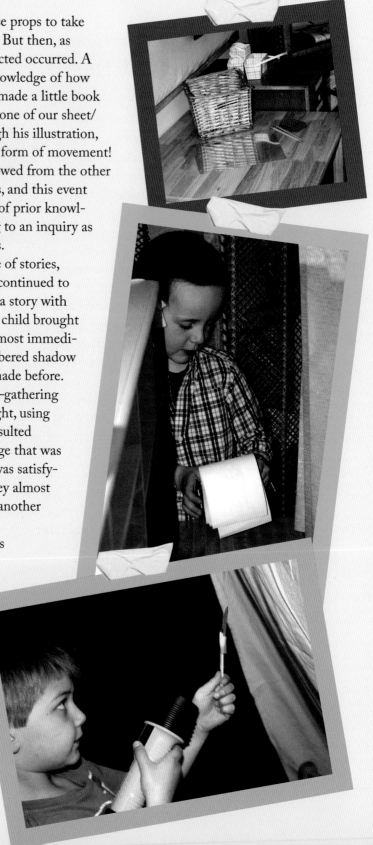

What did this inquiry tell us about the nature of curiosity—both the children's and ours? The children were certainly motivated; this was demonstrated through their determination to surmount challenges and devise strategies to realize their ideas. The materials provided to them were intentional—not too easily providing answers to their challenges but offering pathways to discovery through invitations. We felt curious and yet sometimes confused about the children's thinking: What is it that enables a child to connect between one experience and another? Why did the child who created the flip-book feel that it was necessary to use it behind the screen? It seemed to us that the agency of materials was a key factor and helped us in our role as teacher-researcher, wondering, observing, inviting, experimenting, documenting, and observing again.

Daniel Meier, Gail Perry, Andrew Stremmel, and Barbara Henderson have written extensively on the topic of teacher research and state,

> Children are at the forefront of teacher research. The studies are usually designed to help teachers gain new ways of seeing children, develop deeper understandings of children's feelings and growth, and become more responsive to children. Children's voices are heard through their own words and gestures, photos, drawings, and any other ways by which they are best portrayed. As teachers begin to observe closely, they see children's development played out in their own unique classroom contexts, always influenced by the potentially overlapping cultures of home and school lives. Unlike with conventional educational research, children and families are not just the subjects of research; they are participants and often co-researchers. In this way, teacher research is participatory, inclusive of differences, and democratic in nature. (Henderson et al. 2012)

What Is a Cognitive Knot?

A *cognitive knot* might be described as a "tangle of confusion" (Wien 2008, 152) that teachers and/or children experience when they come up against a perceived problem that seems to impede progress. The problem can help us to reflect deeply in order to determine action. As we explore difficulties with both the children and our colleagues, new possibilities and approaches arise, providing for imaginative, creative responses. In this way, a cognitive knot can ignite excitement about our work and always provides a form of growth.

What Propels Teacher Research?

Put quite simply, curiosity and the questions that arise from this curiosity propel our growth as teacher researchers. Being a teacher researcher puts us into the position of *active learning* along with the children. While most educators value active learning for children, we must also value it for ourselves. Teaching as a form of inquiry enables us to remain active learners, "being a careful observer, a respectful listener, and a thoughtful inquirer about teaching and learning in the classroom. Active learning involves making informed decisions, challenging assumptions, and posing problems" (Hill, Stremmel, and Fu 2005, 47).

Being an inquirer means being able to recognize questions and problems as possible beginnings for creative responses to children and as opportunities rather than challenges. So we might constantly ask ourselves in our inquiry-based environment, "What am I curious about, and how can I find out?"

SOMETHING TO TRY . . .

- Find something within your notes or photographs that puzzles or fascinates you. Take the time to reflect on this event with someone else. What are you curious about? What questions can you raise?

- Consider the ways in your classroom that you can take note of not only what the children are doing and saying, but also your own questions and wonderings.

- Discuss the note/sketchbook from Madeley Nursery School. How might this support teacher understandings and subsequent decision making?

- Search for scripts within your everyday practice. How long have they been in place? Do they work for you? For the children? Are there changes in those scripts that you would like to attempt?

Environments That Make Children's and Teachers' Thinking Visible: Documentation as a Support for Inquiry

When visiting a setting that is new to us, there is something quite wonderful about reading documentation that is either well executed in the form of panels or other formats or still in its raw state, scribbled and sketched, full of questions and wondering. It is enticing and thought provoking, and it helps us to reach understanding of what is going on in this place.

Documentation—the process of making thinking and learning visible through a graphic format—fulfills several roles in an educational setting:

- Through the examination of and reflection upon photographs and notes, before documentation is formally produced, there is the opportunity to deepen our thinking about what took place and how.

During a professional learning event, adults practice looking closely, writing notes, and being in dialogue with others.

- Sometimes we are unsure about children's thinking and ideas, and this perusal and conversation with other educators (and sometimes the children themselves) may lead us to possibilities in terms of what to do next to either support children's ideas and play or find out more about them.

- Curriculum develops as we document, emerging from all the protagonists' questions and curiosities. This curriculum may consist of short or long inquiries, sustained by a series of invitations, conversations, and representations, all documented so we can revisit with both children and colleagues, as well as share with families. Here is an example:

Tadpoles

Here children are discussing the tadpoles in the studio. They talk about what they know and don't know, ask questions of one another, and suggest possible answers. This was a very short exchange captured by the educator at Madeley Nursery School (U.K.) but was offered back to the rest of the group as a way of beginning an inquiry-led project about tadpoles and their habitats.

Amy: "Are they footprints? I don't know."
Beth: "They're frogs."
Amy: "But frogs hop, and they're not."
Beth: "They do look like frogs. They big, big, and big."
Amy: "They all floating. Some are crawling; they have curly things."
Amy: "I didn't think bugs like water . . ."
Amy: "I could ask my sister. She was here; she knows about beetles."
Beth: "They like water."
Amy: "Beetles like water; maybe they are beetles."
Beth: "I can see frogs growing. Frogspawn. They grow up."
Beth: "I see bubbles, frogs in the bubbles."
Beau: "They're tadpoles; they will grow."
Joshua: "I'm drawing froggy water; they all stuck together."

- Documentation, when carefully considered, becomes a form of professional development. We grow as critical thinkers, researchers of children's actions, and members of a community of practice as we think and construct meaning.

- When an inquiry is underway, whether small or large, we want the readers/viewers to understand the children's process in the construction of learning; documentation becomes a powerful communication tool among children and teachers, colleagues, and families.

- Children, through interactions with and about documentation, can think together, clarify, and generate new thinking from the work of others.

- Documentation helps us learn to be in the moment with children and seriously consider their perspectives as we interact, play with them, or simply observe in order to reach understanding.

- When we do not completely understand—which will happen often!—documentation acts as a medium or channel for putting our questions and dilemmas out there for possible responses and input from others. Family members, colleagues, and the children themselves may all respond with their own perspectives. When we do not agree—which will happen often!—the opportunity arises for lively discourse and consideration of many points of view.

- Documentation can act as an archive for an inquiry. Children often move into and out of inquiries, and we need documentation to sustain their curiosity and move forward with investigations. This is particularly useful for children who attend the program part time. They might, for instance, be completely immersed with an inquiry on Tuesday but do not return to the program until Thursday. Documentation can provide a valuable link to their previous play or thinking.

- When inquiries reoccur within a group (for instance, in my teaching career this has happened when children have investigated birds in the winter, only to become curious once again when the birds reappear in the spring), documentation allows us to revisit what we thought before. Do we hold the same views now?

- Documentation, especially with infants and toddlers who cannot yet verbally explain their thinking, often makes children's strategies visible. For instance, how many ways does an infant try to get into an upright cardboard box? And what strategies does the child use to get back out again?

Traces of Thinking: The Importance of Drawing for Young Children

Within any inquiry, whether as simple as how water flows from one place to another or as complex as trying to understand how a text message moves across the world, there is always an opportunity to draw. This becomes an alternate method for understanding and explaining.

As children begin to use graphic representations to make their theories visible, drawing and painting become tools to assist thinking. This can also apply to those children who can already write a little. Drawing might be considered another language for explaining ourselves. As adults we can identify with the idea of understanding how something works through trying to draw it. Our theory of how it might work has to be thought through, probably several times, before we can figure out the parts of the whole and how they all come together. Provisional ideas (how we think it might work at first) give way over time to a more solid understanding. A long time ago, as part of a course I was taking, I was asked to choose a kitchen machine (such as a mixer) and explain through drawing and symbols how it went together and worked. This was tough! But the process helped me think more deeply about the power of graphic representation.

In this day and age, however, when asked to draw their idea, or even to sketch what they've built, many children answer "I can't" or "You draw it for me." It is interesting that children are more likely to try to draw if they are in a relaxed, trusting environment where the teachers' image of the child is that they are certainly capable of drawing when given lots of opportunity, tools, invitations, scaffolding, and time. Chubby pencils in the hands of toddlers result in confident and joyful scribbles that will eventually lead to representations. Preschool children can sometimes "show" rather than "tell" their ideas or theories, as the following drawings by four-year-olds demonstrate:

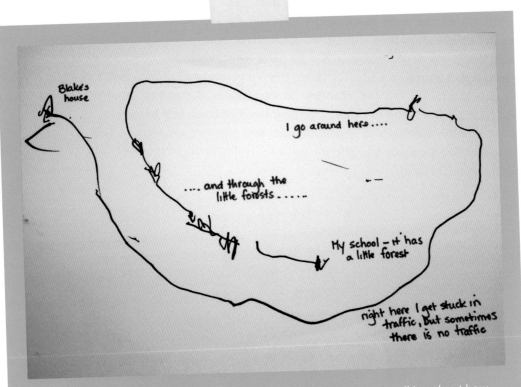

As explained in a previous chapter, a group of preschool children began talking about how to get to school each day. As the conversation evolved, one child had trouble describing how his family drove to school each morning—it was tricky for him to explain verbally yet quite simple when he explained through drawing. Many children noticed this work, and, before long, they too drew maps showing how to get to school. According to their families, these maps were entirely accurate. They also gave us a glimpse of what children actually noticed on this daily travel—"a little forest," for example—and also what was annoying— traffic jams!

Drawing a leaf on the light table provides an opportunity, during an exploration of trees, for the child to really "see" the shape of the leaf as well as its texture. By looking hard, tracing, drawing freehand, and using multimedia, the child becomes able to know the nature of the leaf.

In Reggio schools, drawing is an important activity for children, supported and encouraged by teachers, in describing reactions, theories, beliefs, and opinions. We might refer to this as "drawing to learn, to analyze, to understand" (Janette March, pers. comm. 2017) rather than "learning to draw." For some children, this form of communication can supplement or take the place of verbal language. Sometimes these drawings can be incorporated into documentation. This would be a judgment call on the part of the documenter. Does the drawing support the process and learning you are trying to describe? Does it bring the child's voice more clearly into the documentation? At other times, drawings are simply a valuable tool to enable educators to understand the child's perspective.

Annette Comeau, an early childhood educator and graphic designer, works as a consultant to many early years settings and has frequent opportunities to observe very young children in action with graphic materials. She has been fascinated when watching children initially make a mark, and says, "There is feedback [for the child] from this mark. They will then make another, and another, and it becomes a kind of dialogue, communicating with the self" (pers. comm., 2017).

Pulling Inquiry, Reflection, and Practice Together through Documentation

When Lindsay was a student at the Nova Scotia College of Early Childhood Education, she was fortunate to encounter inquiry-based, emergent practices firsthand at Point Pleasant Child Care Centre during one of her practicum experiences. As part of the college's requirements, she was asked to observe, reflect, and create invitations and experiences based on these reflections and to document them. In other words, Lindsay experienced the cycle of inquiry.

Keeping a journal of her experiences with children—in itself a form of documentation—and thinking about how to respond to children's ideas and actions, Lindsay noted the following:

> Today I noticed S.E. and S.N. playing on the slide outside. They were each holding opposite ends of a large stick and they were sliding down together, with S.E pulling S.N. down the slide with the stick. I stepped in and explained to the girls that I was worried that one of them might get hurt because the stick was so large, and I offered to get some rope so that they could continue to play. I gave them some short lengths of rope. Upon bringing the rope outside the other children also became interested in using it. S.N. and S.E. continued to use the rope to tow each other down the slide. When most of the children lost interest in the rope, I noticed that L.I. and H.C. were now playing on the slide. L.I. had placed a crate on the outside of the slide, stood on the crate, and threw the rope over the side of the slide. I watched as H.C. grabbed the rope and climbed up. Then I observed H.C. grab the rope and slide down. She did this multiple times.
>
> We had previously explored ropes and tying/untying earlier in the morning in the classroom; therefore I believe that this activity was valuable because it allowed the children to experiment with ropes safely and in a different setting. This time they used the ropes primarily as tools to

tow each other up and down the slide. Throughout this activity they used innovation and gross motor skills. I'd be interested in seeing what the children would do with thicker, larger ropes and if they might use those as tools as well.

Lindsay's observation and reflection on her notes did, in fact, lead to an interesting inquiry about knots.

A child, indoors, had been messing about with ribbons, tying them between doors. As an invitation, Lindsay provided a couple of short ropes, simply setting them out to see what would happen. The first child to approach the ropes said, "My dad taught me to how to tie knots," and proceeded to use the ropes for that purpose. He and other children worked on tying them to doors again.

After a few days, this exploration waned a little until Lindsay relaunched the interest with another few ropes, this time tied together as a challenge for children to *untie*. They loved this and asked her to tie knots in "weird ways . . . to make it harder." One child grew from untying two ropes to thirteen. Obviously, he had a thirst for challenge, spending a long time on this, always asking for more, and counting the number of ropes. The ropes he was using were quite stiff, so for variety, Lindsay tried floppy ropes as another invitation, with all the ends tucked in to provide challenge. Again, the child was delighted and told Lindsay, "I'm going to make a spider web at home."

This documentation—consisting of simple notes, a wondering on the educator's behalf, the invitations in response, and one photograph—helps the reader understand the educator's role in supporting inquiry in several ways. The notes enabled Lindsay to think through what happened outdoors and analyze this. Then, to respond not only to children's play but also to her own curiosity, she took the inquiry indoors with similar materials, each providing more of a challenge based on one child's prior knowledge. The noticing of their delight in a challenge was important,

since keeping the children challenged also provided intense motivation to solve these delightful rope puzzles.

What other methods—besides note taking and a camera in the hands of teachers, plus artifacts that children have produced (such as drawings or paintings)—might we use for documenting? Debi Keyte-Hartland, an international consultant who describes her philosophy of working with young children as "being in dialogue with the work of Loris Malaguzzi and the preschools of Reggio Emilia," has worked extensively with educators around the world. She is also influenced by the work of Gregory and Nora Bateson, whose writings shape her thinking about "creating context with children that generates numerous possibilities for describing and constructing ideas and thinking together" (pers. comm. 2017).

Debi was involved in an inquiry process at the International School of Beijing, China. Here she describes how putting cameras in the hands of children provided new insights for teachers and some interesting areas of focus for the children.

Environments That Promote a Culture of Curiosity and Questioning: Photography as a Form of Inquiry

In the classroom, my influences take form in how I work with the concept of inquiry, seeing it as fluid and emergent in process. Importantly, this takes place within a group context where multiple ideas can rise up, become contested, elaborated, and transformed. Children, through their interests and curiosities, take on the mantle of inquirer both as an individual and as a member of a learning group and find questions that they want to pose, create hypotheses, and express their findings to each other. Inquiry, for me, is a process of illuminating thinking where imagination and fantasy are connected to logic and reason and where creativity and expressive dispositions illustrate and connect patterns of thought, aims, and perceptions. The inquiry format, therefore, is not structured but exists as a connected pattern of thought and discovery around a shared idea or question of the group. As the group finds out more, so the collaborative knowledge grows and the group context for research becomes increasingly complex, traveling along multidirectional paths and points of interest.

An example of such an inquiry process was developed at the International School of Beijing, China, and focused upon the medium of photography with their four- to five-year-olds. I offer here a summative story of the exchanges and visual dialogues between the children and their aesthetic research into photography and my interpretation of their learning and curiosity to explore and make meaning. As far as possible, I have tried to create an environment of inquiry where opportunities for creative and critical thinking, together with the communication and expression of their thinking, can be realized and shared, and where learning in relation with others (other children, their families, ourselves as teachers) is a primary principle of being a community of learners.

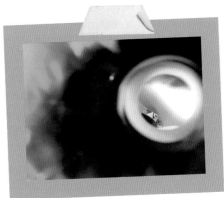

Even before they are born, children are subjects of photography. Babies are scanned before birth, captured in black-and-white tones. With new technologies, babies are increasingly scanned, photographed, and documented in ever more realistic ways. As soon as they are born, photography continues to document and capture their unfolding lives.

As early years teachers, we continue this documentation of children with a focus on how they learn about the world around them, but this inquiry offered an opportunity to find out what happened when we handed the camera over to the children themselves. What would they photograph, where would their gaze dwell, and what would this reveal about photography, the photographer, and their subjects?

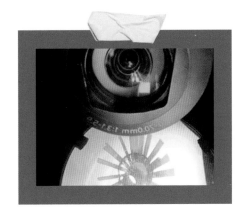

The inquiry began with the children eager to explore the possibilities that the digital cameras offered. Many of the children would take close-ups of the objects and spaces around them, playing with the abstract qualities and images of things. They would also find shapes to photograph through as a frame or fill the entire frame with a specific color or pattern. We could say that this was a form of Pre-Inquiry where children explored cameras and where teachers taught simple skills based on observations of the children.

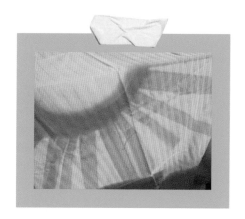

Children were much freer in their use of photography than us as adults. They did not conform with traditional ideas of centrality of subject, symmetry, balance, focus—they experimented and explored and enjoyed the abstract possibilities the camera offered as well as its lifelike representations of subjects. Over time, it was noticed how they photographed things that were curious or important to them. A strong reoccurring feature was the photographs they took of their own block building, and this was highlighted further with the introduction of lights to create shadows of their building work. The children referred to themselves as shadow catchers.

After a period of time, while observing the children and speaking with them about their discoveries regarding light, shadow, and the blocks, the teacher and I reflected on the type of images being taken with the shadows and noticed a further patterning of ideas. This is the point at which possible lines of inquiry begin to take shape. These lines are never solitary but always in relationship to the other possible inquiries.

Many children could be seen to be experimenting with their own shadows, moving their hands to cast shadows and positioning the camera in such a way to capture the image they intended. For me this represented the significant shift children make in their learning from the importance of exploration to one that involves creative and critical thinking. They used their knowledge of the material and tools gained in the exploration stage in an intentional way to express an idea and to communicate meaning.

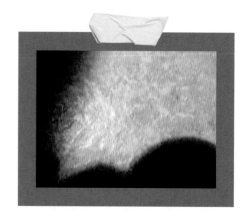

Some children were attracted to shadows that held human form. Maybe this was because they could recognize themselves and their friends' shadows at strange and humorous angles.

For many children, the placement of feet within the frame of the photograph was significant. It was almost as if they were saying, "I am here."

The rainbow effects created by the overhead projector were also constant points of curiosity for the children.

At this point, there were several lines of interrelated inquiry that could have been worked further, with the aim of elaborating and continuing to make complex the children's expression of ideas with the camera. We could have tried to work with all of them, but we felt that it was important for the group of children to continue in their collaborations and group exchanges, as it was providing a rich situation of dialogue and reciprocity of ideas. The work with the shadow people was a strong context where the model who was subject to making the shadows also had a strong creative part to play in the making of the image. I was also reminded by how Carlina Rinaldi said that "pedagogy implies choices, and choosing does not mean deciding what is right compared to what is wrong. Choosing means having the courage of our doubts, of our uncertainties, it means participating in something we take responsibility for" (2006). So it was this particular strand that we took responsibility for in the focused part of the inquiry process.

An offer was made to the children to watch a dance company (Piblious) perform on video a shadow dance. The introduction of information at this stage of the inquiry gave new thought and potentiality to the current ideas of the group. They recognized possibilities within their own work inspired by what they could see in the dance work. New ideas arose; there was a tangible excitement and a new sense of connectedness for the group.

A shadow screen was offered so that children could create and capture moving and still shadows. Children worked both sides of the screen as photographer/director and as performer/shadow maker. There was an increased intentionality to their image making and a renewed effort to collaborate.

Within this focused part of the inquiry, many new themes arose. Images that were scary, images that conveyed pose and balance, and images that merged different bodies as if they were one.

Children in these moments were engaged in a dance of learning within a context that was alive and vibrant to their bodies and their ideas, where the construction of knowledge was mutual and interdependent, imbued with complex relationships between context, materials, the children themselves, and teachers. Children learned within a rhizomatic context, elaborating their ideas in multiple directions and with many possibilities. They made a world of invention around the tool of the camera and turned it into a language that communicated ideas and thinking with intent. Inquiry can so often be turned into a diagrammatic system with boxes and arrows, but this inquiry was organic in nature, growing outward and not through a motionless, boxed-in system, but instead based on relationships of vitality and evolvement. Growth is key, and seeing the process or system of inquiry as one that is as alive and organic as the children themselves. As Nora Bateson posed, "What is the difference between learning and life? None."

There are many enlightening and inspiring aspects of this documentation of children's inquiry with cameras.

First, the cameras themselves become a tool for the children to document whatever it is that interests them: their feet, shadows, and so on. Debi states, "They made a world of invention around the tool of the camera and turned it into a language that communicated ideas and thinking with intent."

Second, the inquiry was entirely organic, with no particular path planned, but rather, educators responded to what was happening while also documenting the children's use of cameras as the inquiry progressed into many tangents. The teachers did not know what would happen but were able to wait and watch.

Third, there were many strands of discoveries, engagement, and interests, and the team—rather than trying to respond to everything that occurred—made some choices about what to pursue with the children. These choices were informed by their philosophy, beliefs, readings (Rinaldi's work, for instance), and questions. After carefully thinking through the children's actions and the teacher's reasoning, these teachers demonstrate intentionality in their decision making rather than choosing arbitrarily.

Documentation in a Bilingual Kindergarten: Sacred Heart School, Sioux Lookout

At the Sacred Heart School in Sioux Lookout, Ontario, there are four kindergarten classrooms, one of which is bilingual (French/English). How does one conduct an inquiry and document it in two languages when the children are just beginning to learn their second language?

Here is a sample of documentation of an inquiry that began with a child's question, deepened into exploration and research, and helped the children reach their own answer—all in two languages:

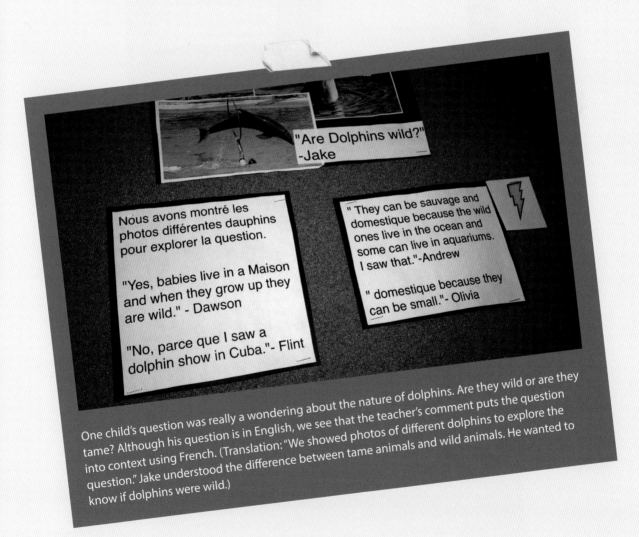

"Are Dolphins wild?" -Jake

Nous avons montré les photos différentes dauphins pour explorer la question.

"Yes, babies live in a Maison and when they grow up they are wild." - Dawson

"No, parce que I saw a dolphin show in Cuba."- Flint

" They can be sauvage and domestique because the wild ones live in the ocean and some can live in aquariums. I saw that."-Andrew

" domestique because they can be small."- Olivia

One child's question was really a wondering about the nature of dolphins. Are they wild or are they tame? Although his question is in English, we see that the teacher's comment puts the question into context using French. (Translation: "We showed photos of different dolphins to explore the question." Jake understood the difference between tame animals and wild animals. He wanted to know if dolphins were wild.)

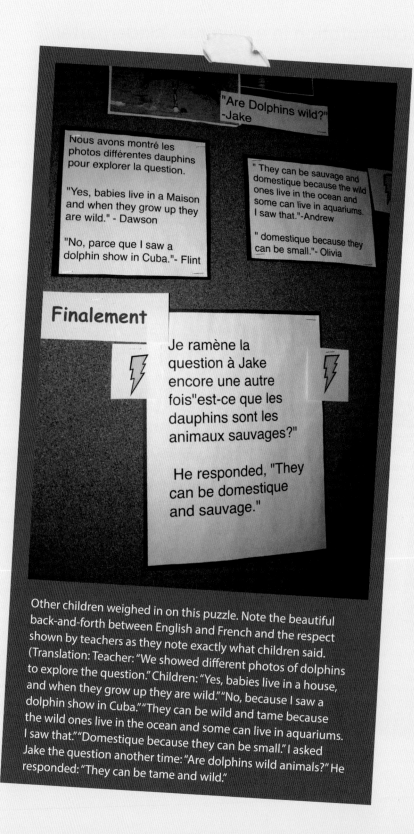

"Are Dolphins wild?" -Jake

Nous avons montré les photos différentes dauphins pour explorer la question.

"Yes, babies live in a Maison and when they grow up they are wild." - Dawson

"No, parce que I saw a dolphin show in Cuba."- Flint

" They can be sauvage and domestique because the wild ones live in the ocean and some can live in aquariums. I saw that."-Andrew

" domestique because they can be small."- Olivia

Finalement

Je ramène la question à Jake encore une autre fois"est-ce que les dauphins sont les animaux sauvages?"

He responded, "They can be domestique and sauvage."

Other children weighed in on this puzzle. Note the beautiful back-and-forth between English and French and the respect shown by teachers as they note exactly what children said. (Translation: Teacher: "We showed different photos of dolphins to explore the question." Children: "Yes, babies live in a house, and when they grow up they are wild." "No, because I saw a dolphin show in Cuba." "They can be wild and tame because the wild ones live in the ocean and some can live in aquariums. I saw that." "Domestique because they can be small." I asked Jake the question another time: "Are dolphins wild animals?" He responded: "They can be tame and wild."

What we see here is a beautiful example of capturing children's theories—their reasoning, discussions, and past experiences—all in two languages, which are interspersed. In bilingual countries, it is common for children and adults to seamlessly flow back and forth between languages, sometimes not even aware of which one they are speaking! These second-language learners insert French when they know the words and comfortably use English when they need to. For the kindergarten team, there is much information here. The children's genuine curiosity produces a question and responses that make absolute sense. Naturally, from their past experiences, they would believe that dolphins contained in an aquarium are "tame." They can, after all, be seen up close and even touched. And there is also a theory that small equals tame and that baby dolphins are different in their wildness from older dolphins. There is plenty to think about within this small piece of documentation.

SOMETHING TO TRY . . .

- If you are already using a particular form of documentation, consider trying another form, such as "raw" documentation that is not intended for display but rather as a thinking tool.

- Examine your existing documentation. How does it support inquiry? How are the children's ideas and thinking made visible? Are teachers' questions included?

- How might you share your documentation with other educators or the community at large? Not everyone is ready for this progression, but if you are, you will gain perspective on your thinking by hearing feedback through another lens. This can be a hugely important part of professional growth.

- Try offering drawing as an everyday tool that children can use to show their thinking. What happens when you offer this possibility to them? How might you use their drawings to help you (and them!) understand their meaning?

An Environment That Supports Teacher Growth

If you have been in the field of early years education for some time, it is interesting to reflect back upon your past practices and think about how far you have traveled, not only in your classroom practice but also in your thinking. We belong to a dynamic profession, one that is constantly changing, responding, and growing to include many perspectives, theories, and, of course, the latest research.

How do we provide an overall environment that provides for the professional growth of teachers? What kinds of work environments encourage staff to explore, grow, speak up about their own ideas, and attempt to remain on the cutting edge of promising practices? Who is responsible for this type of growth?

Sue Fraser, a Canadian educator and coauthor of *Authentic Childhood: Exploring Reggio Emilia in the Classroom*, suggests that the role of the early childhood educator has been steadily changing throughout the twentieth century, explaining, "A hundred years ago, no one would have been able to foresee how much growth and change there would be in early childhood education in the 20th century" (Fraser and Gestwicki 2002, 39).

It stands to reason that if our profession has changed in response to societal changes, then the teacher's role has also changed significantly, and we must be alert to how we keep abreast of what is new, inspiring, and informative within our field. While being alert, however, we do not necessarily have to be accepting; instead we can become critical thinkers, reflecting upon new thinking and our own (informed) point of view.

When considering inquiry-based environments and our own learning within them, we must consider not only what we need to learn but also *how* we learn.

Fraser (45–46), when discussing the role of the teacher in Reggio Emilia, makes the following point:

> Teachers work with one another, with the parents, and with the children to form a "mutual community of learners" among all the protagonists. This means that the children's learning is shared in reciprocal connections. When this basic tenet is understood, other essential components of the teacher's role become obvious, especially the importance of communication. Communicating with children means listening carefully to their ideas and participating with them in conversation. "Listening" may be too simple a word to describe the complex process of attempting to be involved, to follow and enter into the active learning of the child, acting as a resource and sometimes a provoker.

This quote, and indeed the work from within the schools of Reggio Emilia, tell us so much about the inquiry process, the teachers' role within this process, and how it all comes together in a supportive environment:

1. Working as a part of a community of learners

2. Providing for connections, collaboration, and communication between all the protagonists through the art of listening

3. Being both a supporter and a provocateur

4. Being an active learner, walking alongside the children in their learning journey

How do we provide for professional learning in all of these areas? How do we provide or engage in opportunities to be active learners so that we understand not only the theory behind the process of inquiry, but also how these theories might come to life through materials and invitations for the children?

Dispositions

Are you comfortable with being uncomfortable? With learning something new in theory and then trying it out in practice, even though you may not be quite sure of how it will play out? Our dispositions dictate, to a certain extent, how we react to new situations. Some of us embrace change, and some of us avoid it at all costs! If we believe that we are of a certain disposition, such as risk avoidant, are we able to change this disposition? Many educators have found, much to their own surprise, that with support and encouragement, they are able enter into new practices and find a refreshed attitude toward their work.

Sir Ken Robinson, a long-time advocate of change within education systems, contends that there are three types of dispositions when we think about change and creativity within education. He suggests that we might think of people in three ways: those who are immovable, those who are movable, and those who actually move—that is, those people who are eager to learn and motivate others to move along with them. People, of course, don't fit neatly into categories, and as humans we rarely remain static in our attitudes. This provides an opportunity for growth. How do we harness teacher curiosity in order to affect professional growth? How do we turn reticence about change to excitement about what could be?

I believe the answer lies in bringing the focus to the children and to what is best for them. If we come back to the strong capabilities of children, then in our professional learning opportunities, we can seek ways of empowering children so that these capabilities can come to life through inquiry. The initial disequilibrium teachers feel will pass as they relax into this approach, and inquiry can be encouraged and bolstered by others when we work in a supportive environment.

What Is a Supportive Environment for Teachers in Terms of Developing Inquiry?

Let's return to the four points made earlier in this chapter and think about them more deeply in terms of how the workplace setting and the opportunities within that setting can support inquiry and teacher growth:

1. Working as a part of a community of learners

When we are a part of a group of like-minded educators with a shared philosophy and vision, opportunities for lively discussion abound. Whether at staff meetings, on our own time, or online, a community of learners (such as a community of practice) may generate new ideas and thinking by examining documentation and articles or by sharing recent experiences at conferences and workshops, thinking critically about what they have heard and experienced. These communities also often discuss their own classroom practices, either in person or through password-protected social media, a step which in itself leads to reflection. When we trust the group enough to share with them, we need to be able to articulate why we do what we do. Book groups can often provoke these types of discussions. Some groups meet once a month to discuss a particular book chapter by chapter. Inevitably, questions will arise, people will practice some of the approaches they've read about, and they might agree or disagree with the author's opinions. Whatever the result, reading and discussing leads to professional growth in a supportive setting.

What Is a Community of Practice?

A *community of practice*, as described by Wenger, McDermott, and Snyder, "is a group of people who share a concern or a passion for something they do and learn how to do it better as they interact regularly over time" (2002). Such groups of like-minded people gather together on a regular basis to engage in conversation about a particular topic in order to share experiences, learn from one another, and explore resources. In our field, it is so helpful to discuss our practices, vision, challenges, and successes. Through interaction and reflecting with others in a community of practice, we are often able to grow our passions, problem solve, or create new visions for next steps. Communities of practice can be formal or informal groups and are usually quite small in order to facilitate discussion, meeting as often as the group determines will be useful. For instance, one of my own communities of practice is an informal "documentation group." We are a group of people who are deeply engaged with documentation in varied forms, and we share our work with one another once a month. There are lively discussions as we examine different types of documentation, sometimes agreeing and sometimes not, but we are always deepening our thinking and trying new approaches. We support and extend our reflective practices in a friendly and safe environment.

2. Providing for connections, collaboration, and communication among all the protagonists through the art of listening

When engaged in an inquiry with children, how might we enter their world of play, investigation, and curiosity? One of the most important things we can do is to learn how to truly listen.

Carlina Rinaldi thinks about "listening" in many ways, rather than merely hearing children's words. In her work *In Dialogue with Reggio Emilia: Listening, Researching and Learning,* she refers to listening with a series of metaphors: listening as "sensitivity to the patterns that connect"; listening with all our senses rather than with only our ears; listening to the hundreds of ways that children express themselves (as well as their silences!); listening connected to emotions such as curiosity, desire, and doubt; listening as a way to formulate questions rather than answers; and listening as the premise for any learning relationship (2006, 65).

Rinaldi (66) also states, "This capacity for listening and reciprocal expectations, which enables communication and dialogue, is a quality of the mind and of the intelligence, particularly in the young child. It is a quality that demands to be understood and supported. In the metaphorical sense, in fact, children are the greatest listeners of all to the reality that surrounds them."

This deep listening, then, can become a tool for inquiry. When we are *listening* and *noticing* as the events of daily life unfold in the classroom, we open up a window of possibility to enter into the perspective of the child and follow up on that perspective through our responses. This cycle of listening, thinking, and responding can become a habit of being in the classroom, leading to growing expertise on the part of the teacher. Over time the teacher will develop the ability to distinguish between a passing moment of less importance for the child and something that warrants further attention. This is a discrete skill and one that is formed through practice, over time, and through discussion with our colleagues. It is a process of continuous development.

Let's look at an example of this type of listening and noticing in real classroom life:

The child who drew this map of the classroom had a very difficult time transitioning to this play-based classroom. She left her mom with no difficulty, but upon entering the classroom, she seemed "frozen" and unable to make a choice of what to do, no matter how much support and encouragement the teachers offered. She was quite still in the center of the room, simply watching others. She moved only to go to the bath-room or get a snack and would not speak about what she was noticing (although her mom told us she was extremely talkative once she arrived home!). Seeing that she was not upset or particularly uncomfortable, we observed for some days. Other children also tried to invite her to play with no success. We did know, however, that she enjoyed drawing at home and so one day offered pencil and paper to "draw what you like about the classroom."

Her drawing, shown here, told us a lot. What she has included are actually not the areas or choices for play within the room, but the routines—meeting time (shown by square mats), small-group times, the teacher's "messy desk," and so on.

What could we conclude from this? It seemed to us, as we "listened" to this other language from a child who chose not to talk just yet, that she was more comfortable with structured activities (of which there were very few in this particular classroom) rather than the choices available throughout play, which seemed overwhelming to her.

This helped us to help her, putting more emphasis on scaffolding her participation in group times and not worrying about her reluctance to play. In her own time, of course, she did play in all areas of the room with other children, but this took several weeks. In the meantime, she quietly joined us at morning meeting, eventually offering opinions on what she'd seen in the classroom or experienced in her own life.

This kind of listening—which includes listening with empathy, with the heart—reminds us to play close attention to the small clues and actions that children are sending out to us. This, too, helps us develop as teachers, as we learn to include the heart as well as the head in our responses to children and curriculum decisions.

3. Being both a supporter and a provocateur

With children, we fulfill many roles. When working with them on an inquiry, we naturally want to support their ideas and curiosities while not "taking over" their learning. In our field, we long ago moved away from the approach of "transmitting," or seeing children as empty vessels to be filled with knowledge. So how do we support children's ideas and sustain interest without interfering with their innate curiosity, need to play, and willingness to try out new things? Anything we say or do in the classroom has a direct or indirect influence on the children, so *intentionality* should be our goal, keeping our good intentions in mind as we reflect before offering an invitation, an experience, an encounter, or a change in the environment. An invitation is just that—an offering that provides a choice for the child.

The role of teacher as provocateur is an interesting one; we want to provoke a response by offering challenges—perhaps challenges to children's thinking or their approach to using materials. A challenge or provocation should be seen in the positive sense of providing an opportunity to think about something in different ways, of considering a possibility other than the one previously held.

Another word, often used in Reggio Emilia, is *relaunch*—that is, taking a conversation or idea from children and acting as a supporter and provocateur by asking a question that will relaunch and possibly expand their thinking. For instance, the following experience was documented by Reggio educators. When using black, blue, and white crayons in their classroom, children were explaining their drawings to their teacher. After careful listening, the teacher then asked the children, "Can you tell me a story about black, blue, and white?" The children took up this idea, which resulted in multiple stories about the relationships among the three different crayons, with such statements as "See, they are friends; they are touching" and "You can only see the white because the black is there." This last statement, from a four-year-old, is quite astonishing to me. It uncovers the child's knowledge that the white crayon does not show up on white paper unless black or another dark hue is used in contrast. Very thought provoking in terms of what to do next!

4. Being an active learner, walking alongside the children in their learning journey

We often don't know exactly what the children are intending or thinking, but this is fine; as active learners (that is, people who enter into play when invited, who understand the possibility of materials, who are constantly experimenting), we will discover more about the children's thinking as we enter into relationships both with them and the materials they are using. If we think about ourselves as learners alongside them, this will change our teaching practice from reliance on the "all-knowing" educator to a process of discovery. This is a much more exciting stance for us, and it leads to a rich and responsive curriculum for children.

What Should Professional Learning Look Like for This Type of Practice?

When we consider ourselves to be a co-inquirer alongside children, we are speaking of taking the time to look carefully at what they are doing, listening closely for their ideas and thinking, reflecting upon those ideas, and considering many perspectives before responding to them.

Whether you are new to this type of practice or not, it is likely that you will seek professional learning to support your efforts. What types of learning opportunities might be helpful for you? We all differ in terms of how we take in information *and use it*. However, it makes sense that for all of us, if we are interested in expanding our comfort level and growth around the topic of inquiry-based teaching and learning, we need opportunities within conferences, workshops, seminar series, and so on to *practice* those processes and think deeply about them.

Here are some approaches I have used within my own collaborations with teachers and student teachers that have helped them better understand the various contributing factors to inquiry-based teaching and learning:

- Providing opportunities for messing about with materials. When educators, working in small groups of perhaps three or four, use loose parts to explore, wonderful things happen. First, when teachers are given enough time, the possibilities of these materials become apparent. Working alone or with others (collaborating or simply working alongside), we see what others are doing, talk with them as we work, play off one another's ideas, or simply work quietly and alone, deep in thought, or else let our imaginations take flight. These are exactly the types of experiences we would like children to have when they are working with materials. It is also valuable to debrief after the experience in order to reflect on the feelings and understandings that were uncovered during this type of work and to think about how this process of using loose parts ourselves might affect our work with children. For instance, some teachers discover a newfound respect for these materials and their possibilities, leading to increased use of loose parts in the classroom or a better form of organization so that children have easier access to them.

- Observing each other using materials. As educators, we might say that we are skilled observers, having learned observation approaches during our training or else being in the habit of regularly observing children in the classroom. However, what exactly are we paying attention to? What are we noticing? According to Dr. Carol Anne Wien, we tend to "observe what we know" (pers. comm., 2016). That is, when we are in a familiar setting with familiar children, we may have an expectation, from experience, of what will occur and what it means. To break out of this script, it is useful to practice observing out of our comfort zone. By having two adults explore and play with loose parts while a third educator is watching, listening, and taking notes (but not intervening or commenting!), we create a sense of truly seeing. Afterward, as the writer debriefs what she has paid attention to and written, very interesting dialogues occur as all three people explain their thinking and/or actions. This is a reminder that we need to pay attention to the small things that occur during play, the puzzles we have about those events, and the conversations taking place as the play unfolds. Also, we are reminded to keep an open and flexible mindset as we observe and then interpret. This is the beauty of working within a team—we consider all perspectives, and they may all be different. This gives us the chance to discuss further, to clarify others' meanings, and to articulate our own point of view before making a decision and moving forward.

- Providing the opportunity to ask bigger questions. As previously mentioned, our focus need not be only on developmental domains. How can we practice asking "bigger" questions? One approach is to respond to a video clip (either from the educators' own setting or from those made available for this purpose, such as Dr. George Forman's Videatives series) and have an initial dialogue with other participants in the workshop, or team members if in your own setting, about what happened. It is likely that everyone will have noticed different aspects of the event. After everyone's perspective

After spending much time building a tree house in the classroom, the children were invited to draw it before it was taken down. I wondered what their drawings would look like and how they would differ since they were surrounding the structure, all drawing from different perspectives. As I looked at their drawings afterward, I could have focused on their representational skills, which were considerable. But instead I wondered, "How does drawing from different perspectives change the child's understanding of the object?" This is a bigger question, and since these particular children loved to draw, it was a one that I was able to pursue by offering many objects, on several occasions, to draw from different angles. The children themselves began to notice significant differences in their drawings, and we were able to begin discussing "point of view" in the literal sense.

has been heard, it is time to raise some questions about the event, striving to "think big."

Sometimes when we examine photographs or videos of our children in action, we need a provocateur to move our thinking forward a little, asking us for more.

Liz Hicks is an experienced consultant who works with educators all over the eastern provinces of Canada, often in settings that identify themselves as emergent, inquiry based, or Reggio inspired. Here is how she responded when asked about her role of provocateur:

> I am always amazed at how people value the role I play as a "provocateur," "consultant," "critical friend" when I myself often wonder if I make any impact at all! Some educators tell me that my role keeps them on track and helps them look at children's ideas, play, or work in a different way and helps to give their work more meaning. I always enjoy the conversations . . . especially when educators are passionate about telling the stories of what children are bringing their attention to and what educators are wondering about, what is drawing their attention.
>
> In one center I work with, I attend a classroom team meeting every other week. I always try to observe the morning or day before the team meeting—observing the children at play (not educators, unless I have been asked by an educator to give feedback on a particular concern, etc.). I also read their posted program plans, reflections, and documentation, making notes on any "themes of thought" on the children's or teachers' part (or "traces" as they say in Reggio Emilia) that seem to pop up, winding their way through their notes.
>
> I am fortunate to have worked with this particular center for a few years now, and I have built strong relationships with all staff. This is a very important component of my work.
>
> At the team meetings, we usually work with the "Thinking Lens"—developed by Margie Carter, Deb Curtis, and Ann Pelo—to reflect on anecdotal notes and photographs that staff bring to the meetings. I have noticed over the years we do not need to reference these as much, as it has become part of our script to think in this way, unless it is a new team.
>
> There are times when staff do not bring observations, etc. In some cases, staff rarely bring artifacts. This can be a challenge—however much I encourage and show the benefits. In this situation, I ask about what has caught their attention, or something I have observed or have noticed mentioned on their program plans, and then move into the questions using the Thinking Lens.

I also use my own observations and photographs as a launching pad for discussion.

Other techniques/questions I have used are:

- Open-ended questions, discussing feelings, "What is exciting you at present?" "Tell me about," "Tell me what you have been doing," "What is it about these actions that intrigued you or you wanted to try?"

- I see that you added _____ to the _____ area. How did you introduce those materials? What guided your decision to add them to the area?

- I was wondering what was going on when the children in the _____ area were . . .

- I wonder how . . .

- I wrote an observation note about _____ today. Let's talk about what I saw—I am wondering what insights you may have about what was happening or s/he was thinking about . . .

- I'd really like to know more about . . .

- What would happen if . . . ?

- What's your best guess about what is happening?

- Why do you think that happened?

- You seemed to enjoy . . .

One of my greatest challenges is slowing educators down—from jumping to the "big" idea too quickly or wanting to create something—or assuming that an activity (perhaps one from Pinterest!) is the next step. We live in a world of quick fixes, or of needing a product to prove our worth, or to show that children are "doing something." The greatest value in our work is to look and listen closely, to take time to think with others about what is drawing the children's attention and what could be the next steps to deepen the wonder and joy in what they are seeing, doing, and discovering. (pers. comm., 2017)

Mind maps have been around for a very long time, yet I still find them to be a highly useful tool that empowers people to "get at" all their prior knowledge and then think about the effects of each of these pieces by drawing connecting lines, symbols, and questions.

Below is an example of a very rough map developed by student educators in one of my classes. I asked them to think about what they knew in terms of the connections between emergent curriculum and documentation. This map is very messy, just as the process of thinking is sometimes messy!

What Are Mind Maps?

Although organizational diagrams have been around for centuries, it was Tony Buzan in the United Kingdom who popularized this form of mapping knowledge as a way of organizing our thoughts.

A mind map is a visual tool organized around a central idea or word. From this central word or phrase (for instance, *drawing*), one draws thick lines as tangents, spreading outward, leading to more ideas. So, in the case of *drawing*, these lines might represent "learning through drawing, drawing as representation, drawing as a language," and so on. These words—your initial ideas around drawing—are written along the thick lines.

Then, as more thoughts occur around the topic, finer lines are drawn, again spreading outward. Some people like to use different colors for different areas of thought. As you progress with your thinking, the map will become more and more complex and connections will become apparent, producing even more lines.

What we end up with is a map of our prior knowledge, our thinking around the topic, and new ideas that crop up as we work.

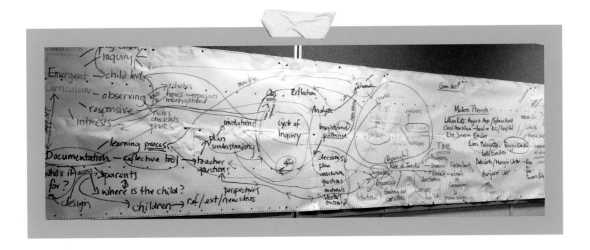

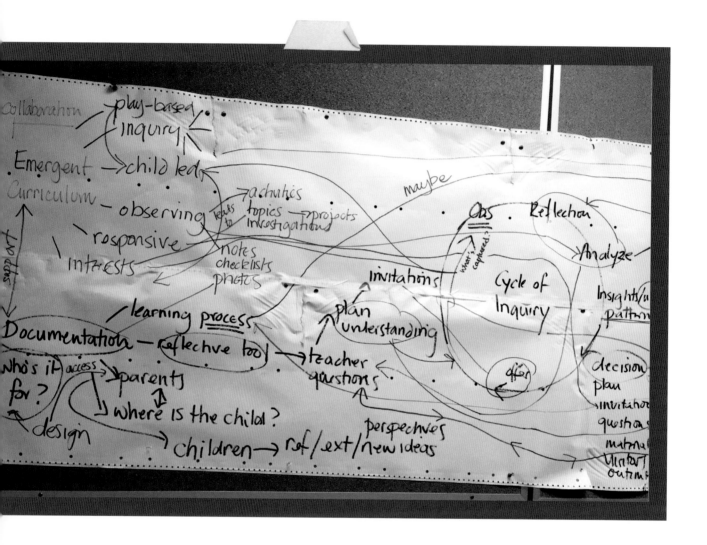

You can see the connections that people are making: the connections between emergent curriculum and documentation; the ways that these approaches affect practice; the image of the child, inquiry, and theorists behind these approaches; the influence of Reggio Emilia; and so on. In fact this was an overview/revisiting of everything we had learned within our course!

During an inquiry by children, a mind map is another tool for educators to make sense of and organize everything that is happening—the protagonists' thinking, the learning taking place, and future possibilities.

Collaborations between educators, consultants, workshop presenters, or pedagogical leaders should be ongoing in order to be of use. In my experience, a "one-shot" workshop—no matter how inspiring—is often of little use in practice if there is no follow-up. Therefore, a series of workshops building upon participants' experiences as they emerge in their classrooms is very valuable. Many consultants now offer an initial workshop or seminar to introduce and explore a topic, and then the participants go back to their settings for two or three weeks to experiment with new-to-them approaches. When they reconvene, they are not only able to discuss successes and/or struggles, but sometimes they also bring along data in the form of photographs, which can be further developed into documentation.

Another way to follow up on the first workshops and ensuing experimentation is to connect online through Skype, FaceTime, GoToMeeting, or another medium. Having teachers and pedagogical consultants or workshop leaders come together as a group online for an hour during a team meeting or whole-center discussion can be invaluable in terms of offering reassurance, answering lingering questions, and brainstorming further strategies. Book study groups sometimes use this "virtual discussion" format to connect with the author or consultant to further discuss or uncover ideas that the book has provoked.

What is it, after all our study, reading, and professional learning through discussion and reflection, that we are trying to achieve? Certainly we are not searching for facts to remember. In our society, facts can change in a heartbeat as research and knowledge are shared at a rapid pace. Instead we might strive for the development of growth in our thinking, brought about by opportunities to hear about, see, and experience innovative approaches to our work. We can also strive for the development of a certain frame of mind that is open to possibilities; this may feel like risk taking in terms of what might happen in the classroom, but it also engenders an attitude of excitement and passion for our work. Perhaps thinking about teaching as inquiry will enable you to embrace the role of question-asker and problem-poser rather than a holder of knowledge.

Here is an example from a preschool educator who made a huge shift in thinking on her journey to embracing inquiry.

Making the Shift from Scripted to Inquiry-Based Practice: A Conversation with Linda, Small World

When you have worked in a more "traditional" or themed way in the past and then join an organization that works with inquiry-based practices, how do you make that shift in thinking and practice, and how does it feel?

Linda had trained at a college that emphasized play-based learning. She understood, engaged with, and bought into this philosophy. However, once she entered the field, there were expectations—sometimes from centers themselves and often from families—to focus more on academics. This made her feel uncomfortable, as if she was not being true to her own philosophy.

Some years later, Linda joined Small World Learning Centre in Bridgewater, Nova Scotia. This center, led by Donna Stapleton, is very much inspired by the work in Reggio Emilia and Malaguzzi's theories. Here Linda was not only given permission to focus on play and inquiry but was actively encouraged by Donna to do so. The feeling of pressure disappeared, and she was able to relax into her practice.

Linda states, "It comes back to the image of the child; being able to 'let go' and believe in the child, trust them, and I also realized I didn't always have to be in control—that they can lead. I could relax, and joy happened. Now, I think to myself, 'What do they know?' and 'What's my role in this?'"

She remembers returning from vacation and being greeted by a boy with whom she'd worked closely and formed a strong relationship. He excitedly pulled her to his cubby to show her a rock, which he said "looks like a dinosaur, and I can paint it." This small moment told Linda many things. After some initial struggles when first attending the setting, this child now trusted his educator and—hugely for him—was able to "see beyond" the concrete object to imagine what it might be, seeing something else through the lens of his imagination. For Linda this was a moment when she realized that with relationship and an open environment—open about thinking as well as about the use of materials—children can come to imagine what might be. This moment could be taken and developed into a larger investigation, yet it is valuable just in itself. The child's thinking has grown, and, through relationship, Linda was a part of that growth.

This imaginative lens has spread into other areas of the routines at the center. For example, when a child spills milk at lunchtime, there is not a frantic rush to immediately clean it up, but there is a pause to ask, "Hmmm . . . what does that look like?" It's an entirely different way of being in the classroom!

SOMETHING TO TRY . . .

- Together with your teaching team or staff, consider how you make decisions about the nature of your professional learning. What do you learn from these events or series that you are able to take back to your setting and actually use? What are some other options other than those you have already tried? An example might be bringing in a consultant, coach, or mentor to work alongside you, rather than always attending workshops. If workshops are useful to you and you learn from them, consider what types of learning experiences within these workshops work for you and why.

- Choose an aspect of your practice that you feel might benefit from change or growth on your part. What would be some small steps you could take to begin this process?

- With your team or the whole staff, identify how your organization provides for connections, collaboration, and communication. Try a mind map to help visualize how these facets interconnect.

An Environment That Nurtures and Supports Relationships

Imagine entering a classroom each day knowing that whatever idea or challenge or investigation that you are engaged in will be supported—supported by the people around you, the environment in which you are immersed, and the materials that are available to you. What difference would this make to you as a child or as a teacher? Both children and teachers need to be in an environment of supportive relationships if they are to fully investigate their ideas, using encounters with people and materials to grow and learn.

Within an emergent, inquiry-based classroom, we are ideally all in collaboration with one another and value both independence and collaboration, seeing each as necessary and contributing to the creative act of early education. As teachers we strive to notice and value independent thoughts and actions, paying attention to each child's thinking. At the same time, we see connections among children as they become curious about others' play, experiment with materials, and begin to interact with one another. In some early years settings, educators make a conscious effort to bring children's thinking to the attention of other children in order to provoke further ideas or to simply help them consider the point of view of others.

When we as teachers comment thoughtfully on children's play or examine documentation with children, this type of response often becomes contagious. A three-and-a-half-year-old in one of my classrooms, for instance, offered this comment when looking at another child's drawing: "I really like the way it's all over the page. And I wonder what this bit is about" (pointing). This comment was almost like listening to myself in conversation with children! They are listening to us all the time, and our modeled curiosity is indeed caught up and used by them.

Children in Relationship with Teachers

What do each of these protagonists bring to the idea of inquiry and to teaching and learning? And what is the teacher's role in this relationship?

When you think about the nature of childhood and your personal image of children, what comes to mind? We think of children as curious, capable, investigative individuals who bring a great deal of prior knowledge to us through their life outside of the classroom, including their families, community, and culture. Once they become articulate, children have many questions. And children who do not yet speak also have many ways of communicating their knowledge and curiosity through what they pay attention to, what engages them, and their body and facial languages.

What is your image of the teacher? What is this person there to do? Old scripts for teaching involved the stance of "transmitter of knowledge," yet we know this is not the case in modern thinking and in emergent, inquiry-based practices. In order for us to be in supportive relationships with children, we must have an idea of our roles in this type of classroom.

How do we form relationships that nurture curiosity and follow up with inquiry? And what do we actually *do*?

I recently had the pleasure of hosting Dr. Carol Anne Wien in my Emergent Curriculum and Documentation course at the Nova Scotia College of Early Childhood Education to speak about the role of the teacher in the schools of Reggio Emilia. Beginning with "the image of children as competent, capable, rich in potential, and expert meaning-makers of their own experience," Dr. Wien went on to discuss several roles for the teacher:

- Listener—following the connections that children are making
- Creator of contexts—structuring the environment to engage children in play and design
- Documenter—mirroring children's thoughts and feelings back to them, revisiting these thoughts in order to allow new ones to emerge, sharing with colleagues and the broader community
- Converser—thinking together with the children, theorizing about the world
- Researcher—inquiring into and attempting to understand children's thinking, learning as co-inquirer, thinking of studio work as research into materials (not "art")
- Creator of pleasure—considering aesthetic qualities such as beauty, joy, and positive feeling in being alive

Dr. Wien says, "The stance of the teacher, to my mind, is one of empathic responsiveness encompassing qualities such as authenticity in adults (not scripted talk), attentiveness (close and careful listening to the children), and appreciation for children's intentions and attempts to learn" (pers. comm., 2016).

Let's pause to think further about how a relationship involving "empathetic responses" to children would support their inquiries. The infant would quickly come to trust an empathetic and careful observer to meet his or her needs—not only physical and emotional needs, but also the need for stimulation, exploration, and exposure to new and interesting materials and events. The toddler, just beginning to articulate needs and thoughts as well as assert a shaky independence, would be provided with a sensitive and thoughtful response, even though this child may not completely understand what he or she really wants! The preschool child (and older) has the ability to express ideas as well as understandings and misunderstandings. What a wonderful relationship it would be if all of these young children were able to enter into a conversation with someone who takes their thinking seriously, takes the time to consider it, and then responds thoughtfully. These are reciprocal relationships where everyone has a voice and is heard.

In Relationship with Materials

When we think of materials, we think about inanimate objects or objects that can begin as inanimate and transform into something else in the child's mind. Blocks can become creatures, for instance, and wire can become a person. So how do materials speak to us? How do children form a relationship with materials?

To understand this, we must first understand that materials—whether they are continuous (that is, able to change shape and re-form), such as sand or water, or discontinuous (that is, static in their form), such as blocks or play animals—have what we refer to as *agency*. This means they have an effect and provide a kind of provocation. They are *active* agents in the formation of our understanding of the world—we make things or express ideas with them, and those things have an effect on us.

During a recent discussion about the agency of materials, Matthew Sampson, an experienced educator and master's student, commented on the meeting of children and materials. He likened this to the child "bringing all of her prior knowledge and experiences to this meeting, then engaging with the material, and then—on the other side of this encounter—new openings and directions and possibilities occurring as understandings develop" (pers. comm., 2017).

Using Encounters with Materials as a Form of Inquiry

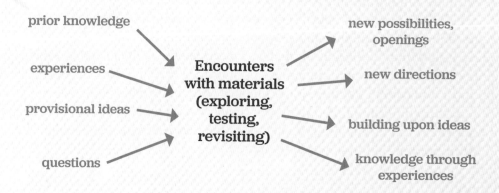

In Reggio Emilia, considerable thought is given to the areas of relationship and to materials and how they are presented. In *Authentic Childhood*, Susan Fraser tells us that "teachers in Reggio inspired classrooms no longer set up materials in isolation; instead, they think carefully about the interconnection between materials and children, and how this relationship deepens the meaning of activities" (Fraser and Gestwicki 2002, 89).

A way of describing this careful attention to materials and their relationship with children might be *intentional*. Nothing enters the environment that is not carefully considered. The materials are there for a reason, whether that reason is a repeated playful engagement from the children, an invitation from the teachers that may provide for further investigation from the children, new items that tie in to their thinking, or something challenging that will provoke discussion.

The Role of the Atelier

One of the most intriguing and thought-provoking areas of practice that Reggio Emilia has shared with us is that of the *atelier*. Roughly translated as "studio" or "workshop," an atelier might be thought of as a workshop for ideas. This space—sometimes within the classroom or, if we are very fortunate, a separate space—is a place for a wide array of interesting materials that respond, provoke, and sustain the ideas and thinking of children. Around the world, educators have responded to the idea of ateliers with great enthusiasm and intense interest. Naturally any physical space will represent the philosophy of those who created it, and so ateliers differ—as they should. Yet they share some common aspects.

Atelierista Vea Vecchi describes the ateliers in Reggio Emilia:

> The atelier is a place that guarantees that knowledge and learning are taking place with the mind and with the hand, as well as rationality and emotions connected. The atelier is also a physical place where products are conceived and produced using different materials and techniques. It is a place where the authors of these products are children and youth working alongside adults who have learned how to listen . . . teachers who support the children as they are carrying out their own research, listening to the questions that the children ask themselves . . . teachers who try not to impose their own ideas on the children . . . teachers who allow the children to be the protagonists of their own imaginations and their own strategies for learning as much as possible. (2012)

Vecchi goes on to speak of the empathetic relationship that children have with the world around them. So, we come back to relationships with materials and with the world at large and to careful listening.

During a recent study tour in Reggio Emilia, I was intrigued as an atelierista spoke of the atelier as having a vibration that flows through the school like an infusion. Around the world, we see children explore materials in their classrooms, carry out in-depth work in the atelier in small groups, and then take this work back to the classroom for further exploration—creating a relationship between the small group and the larger group and between materials in one area and another. Inquiry flourishes as we all learn how to approach and consider materials in many different ways, in different spaces, and with different people. We might think of ateliers as a place of provocation to explore further, connect ideas, and listen to one another and to what the materials suggest. And if you do not have the luxury of a separate space for this type of work with materials, don't worry. There are multiple ways to create a nook, corner, or central space for inquiry with materials. Here is an example:

In Relationship with Parents and the Community: Revisiting the Role of Documentation

How does inquiry-based work bring parents into the classroom community? How do we best make our work with their children a partnership with parents and caregivers? And how does the wider community at large become enticed and interested in the work?

Documentation as Communication

Documentation, in all its forms, has become a major method of communication with families. Whether a hard copy displayed within the classroom and hallways or digital documentation that is sent home, it is a valuable resource for parents. By reading documentation that includes both children's and teachers' thinking about play and investigations within the classroom, and by being invited to comment on what they read, parents become an integral part of the classroom environment.

In order to contribute, parents need to be invited and encouraged to share their thoughts (not only about their own children, but also about teaching and learning as a whole), their reactions to projects and small moments, their questions and puzzles about why we do what we do, and their possible contributions if they are able to come into the classroom to spend some time with us. These comments and experiences from parents can be used as a part of ongoing documentation and are likely to draw other parents in.

In the introduction of *Documenting Children's Meaning: Engaging in Design and Creativity with Children and Families,* Jason Avery, Karyn Callaghan, and Dr. Carol Anne Wien describe their book as "a portrait of a way of living with children so that they and their families share in high quality experiences that expand identity, authenticity, and loveliness that can be daily living, and the creativity and imagination that children bring to life in our world. One of the things we love about this book is the strong presence of families, and their willingness to be visible alongside their children" (2016, 3).

There are indeed many lovely examples of "being alongside their children" in their book, and the photographs were taken in a part-time family resource program where a diverse group of children and their caregivers drop in from time to time. The somewhat transient and very part-time attendance of this widely mixed age group might be seen by many educators as a huge challenge in terms of documentation. Yet it is the documentation that anchors the program, because the children can come back after a few days and revisit what they were so engaged with the last time they were present. According to the authors, the documentation "carries ideas forward" (2016, 7), and we can see that this use of documentation would be very useful to all part-day programs.

Documentation as a Form of Research with Parents

When we document ideas and questions (rather than simply "what happened"), and when we share this documentation in discussion with families, we are on a quest together to find out more about what the children are doing and why, about the teachers' thinking and responses, about the parents' responses, and about the materials in the environment and their effects. All of the questions that we ask of ourselves and that are generated by others can be researched within our daily practice with children. We may not be quite sure of what to do next, but reading through children's words and actions will give us clues. We become detectives searching for just the right response, perhaps in the form of an invitation that will provide more information or another conversation as we examine photographs with children and parents and embrace their input.

Documentation in the Wider Community

I often take part in discussions in which early years educators—including myself!—bemoan the fact that few people outside of our own profession understand what we do and why we do things in a particular way. We would love for the general public, especially in our own communities, to understand the depth of thought and care that goes into our daily work with our youngest citizens—how we reflect carefully before acting, how we value play, and why. And we especially want the community to understand the competence of young children, which they demonstrate by their theories, either verbally or in graphic forms, of how the world works. We would love for their thinking and ideas to be given the respect that they deserve.

It is my belief that we can achieve some of these goals by spreading documentation throughout our communities. While it is becoming more and more commonplace to find quality documentation of inquiries within early years settings, it is still uncommon, at least in North America, to see documentation in public spaces.

For instance, we can envision the effect of documentation in public libraries, doctor's offices, ferry terminals, and so on. For the public to read children's explanations of how something works would surely engender respect for their quality of thinking, their imaginative ideas, and the logic that they bring to the puzzles of daily life. We want and need this respect for children and for our work with them.

For many years, the teachers in Reggio Emilia have been in relationship with their wider community. Local city officials, retailers, businesspeople, and others all see the work of the children around the city (for instance, in the pedestrian tunnels and in restaurants) and understand what goes on within these schools.

I invite you to consider the wider sense of the word *environment* when considering the sharing of documentation and to explore ways of sharing the important work that children and early educators are doing together.

SOMETHING TO TRY . . .

- Write down what actually happens during a typical day in your setting; however, instead of focusing on routines (such as snack or rest time), itemize those aspects of your day that you consider "program" or "curriculum." What does this list say to you about your enactment of your philosophy and beliefs?

- Individually note what you believe your role to be in the classroom.

- Now allow yourself to dream! What would you love to be doing with children that isn't happening or that you think cannot happen? Think big! What gets in the way of your dreams? How could you make some of these things happen in even some small way?

- Photograph several views of your art area/atelier. Consider these photographs with your team. What messages does this area send to children?

Inquiry in Action—Creating Brave Spaces

> "Learning to be still and present have been two of the most meaningful tools that I have used in my experience as being a witness to another person's story."
>
> –S. J. JONES

Would you have an idea of how to explore the world of "real versus not real" with four-year-olds? What alive or dead means? The difference between alive and real? Would you know where to begin, or would you wonder whether you should explore these topics at all? This was the situation that a team of three educators faced at Point Pleasant Child Care Centre in Halifax, Nova Scotia.

This inquiry is included here for several reasons; most importantly it shares the discomfort that the educators felt from time to time—the "not knowing" or not being quite sure of what to do next. Yet we see that they also learned how to move on from this feeling of disequilibrium. This example also offers an opportunity to see the cycle of inquiry unfold: the careful listening and noticing, the writing of rough notes for reflection, the decision-making process in terms of what to do next, and then observing again. Relationships and trust, in particular, are highly visible. This includes relationships among the team members themselves and between children and educators. Most of the elements of inquiry from this book, in fact, are present here.

Brave Spaces: An Inquiry with Four-Year-Olds

Introducing the Educators

S. J., Aya, and B. were a newly assembled team at the time of this inquiry, and for two of them, this was their first teaching position. Aya had worked for three and a half years at this centre, but S. J. and B. had only recently graduated from a two-year ECE program, which Aya had also previously attended. This shared educational experience at least gave them the possibility of a cohesive philosophy and a starting point for sharing beliefs and approaches. As is evident from their words below, though, even with this background, the team had many differences.

S. J. begins:

Since the beginning of my journey as an early childhood educator, I have set out to collect the diverse stories and perspectives that have molded the people in my community. Working with children and families has been a test of my ability to witness life in its unfiltered, unedited form. Before obtaining my early childhood education diploma, I worked as a dancer and theater artist. My professional training in the realm of performing arts heightened my curiosity about human interaction, specifically in regard to fostering an imaginative and intuitive culture within a collective. During my schooling as an early childhood educator, I discovered that I was particularly drawn to the teachings about classroom cultures and the significance of the environment on the children's, educator's, and the greater community's learning. More and more I wanted to know what it looked like and felt like to intentionally develop a space where each person was seen and heard, and where the physical environment reflected the collective's values right back at them.

In my initial months fresh out of school, I felt overwhelmed with theory and suggestions about best practice. When I finally stood alongside my two new coworkers and we looked at the twenty-three children that would be in our care, I wondered which classes had best prepared me for this scenario. I was terrified. I remembered Emily Martinello, one of my teachers at the college, saying, "Everyone is always doing the best they can with what they have."

I knew I could listen, so I started there.

B. comments on her own background:

Challenge accepted! That's what I said to myself when I said yes to the job offer at Point Pleasant Child Care Centre. I challenged myself to work in an organization that is known for its excellent commitment in the early childhood education field. I challenged myself to work in an age group that I had only known in theory and with an age group that was already well versed in the English language with ideas and imagination soaring up high. Will I be able to keep up with them knowing that English is not my first language? I took the challenge to work with individuals who are "newbies," not to mention that all three of us came from different cultures, race, identities, value systems, philosophies, and beliefs.

Previously I had worked for over eight years as a social worker in the Philippines. I had committed myself to work for people who were in dire need of support, love, and care. The background I had was deeply rooted with family dynamics and children. This is why I chose to take on this profession of early childhood education.

During my early months at the college, I was having difficulty adjusting and opening up myself because of my culture and family beliefs, which I felt were the total opposite of what I had been learning and experiencing in my previous work. In social work, we were intended to practice individuality and to engage in the belief to work to the best interest of each person. Also we worked as a team of multiple individuals coming from different professions, backgrounds, and experiences. All of these experiences from my past came together, and over time I was able to work my way through ECE life here in North America.

Aya shares previous experiences:

My interest in early childhood education started since my child, Aidan, was born. I was so curious about how this small human grows and how I can support him to be the best he can be. This interest brought me to Nova Scotia College of Early Childhood Education. Through the years, I became fascinated about how to set up a table activity for children to enhance certain skills without my guidance. I was also interested in project work with children and effective documentation for children, teacher, and parents. Susan was my contact teacher at one of my practicum sites, and I was seeing how preprimary children can be involved in projects and can join in group discussions. What the children discussed really impressed me. Since I graduated, I've been working at Point Pleasant Child Care Centre, where I've been experimenting with documentation methods.

Like other early childhood educators, I encountered issues with how to make parents read and find time to do documentation. With S. J. and B., I found a really effective way to do documentation that helped to increase the depth of projects with children. Before I came to Canada, I studied artificial intelligence in university, specializing in visualizing the structures of high-dimensional data. I see similarities between artificial networks and what happens in our minds, although humans have much more flexibility. Through my study, I became interested in how intelligence works and grows. That's why working with children has been really fascinating and exciting for me.

The Formation of Relationships

S. J., B., and Aya realized that they must first form a relationship with one another before they could work effectively together and reflect upon children's ideas and actions. Here, in their words, is how they formed a trusting relationship that would, in the future, underpin their confidence in taking on a "risky" inquiry:

S. J. talks about the teachers' relationships and forming a "triangle of vulnerability":

When it was solidified that I would be working in the preprimary classroom alongside Aya and B., I was reminded of what it felt like to be cast in a performance alongside other actors I didn't know. I remember thinking in my past career, and then again in my current one, "Will I be good enough?" but this had more weight than any show I had ever performed in. We would be nurturing other people's children together. This seemed daunting. *We MUST get along. We MUST be on the same page. We MUST enjoy one another.* This is what I thought at the time, and I think this is what drove me to wanting to know my two coworkers as deeply and completely as they would let me.

Over the summer months leading up to the beginning of the fall term with our new group of four-year-olds, the three of us met as often as we could over dinner and drinks. We are from three very different cultures and countries, we speak four languages, we follow different diets, we believe in different Gods, we are diverse in gender, orientation, and the color of our skin. And despite all of these potential challenges, we found common ground. At first, we timidly disagreed with one another from time to time. But as we grew closer, we relished in tearing apart our traditional beliefs of what a teacher ought to be. We slowly allowed ourselves to be vulnerable, and it was in our moments of vulnerability with each other, whether at a restaurant or in the classroom, wherein we built a trusting foundation that allowed us to be our authentic selves when interacting with the children. We found ways to bring that vulnerability to the forefront. An example of this occurred when we first inherited our classroom from a disbanded teaching team. In an almost ritualistic manner, we met in that classroom over a weekend, meticulously looking at everything in the space, from furniture to materials and even to the plants that were left behind. We debated over each item: could it live in our new space? The criteria was that if it was not either incredibly useful or incredibly beautiful, then it had to go (Kondo 2014). We had to dig deep to debate our feelings about such inanimate objects as lamps and stools. However, as long as the process was, we managed to create a place that each of us could call home for the next year. The environment celebrated us as individuals but also as a collective, while inviting the children to explore and make their own contributions.

During my theater training, we learned all sorts of relational exercises to connect us to each other and to the space we happen to be inhabiting. One of these exercises involved choosing two other people in the space. One person you were meant to follow, and the other person you were supposed to stay away from. The hard part was that you had to try and keep the one you were following and the one you were staying away from in equal distance to your own body. Usually twenty people were involved in this experience, and each person was following and staying away from their own two chosen people. As a group, we were asked to walk, everyone moving to the place they needed to be to keep the distance between themselves and their chosen others equal, essentially forming a perfect equilateral triangle. This, of course, was almost impossible to achieve because each step would set off a chain reaction of everyone else trying to maintain their triangles. This has been an important metaphor for my relationships with Aya and B. I often think of them as the two I chose to follow and stay away from. I always keep them at an equal distance, desperately trying to keep our values, wants, and needs in balance. I can feel when our triangle turns into more of an acute or isosceles shape when I follow one of them too much and stray from the other. It's a constant readjusting, and outside forces always interfere and pose obstacles. But when we form that perfect triangle, there is a sweet spot where we are real, when we can be *still* and *present*. That is when we are at our best. We have come to know this triangle as our *Brave Space*.

B. gives a point of view on relationship building:

I mentioned earlier that we are diverse teachers. Apart from our differences, the challenge was that we rarely had opportunities to get to know each other and work together over the summer before our in-depth work with children began. However, these circumstances were not taken as a negative, because we met for dinner after work. During those meetings, we not only talked about our classroom but also about our lives outside of work. We had several meet-up nights full of fun, laughter, agreement, and disagreement. However, despite the differences that we had, we became one in our desire to be *intentional* in our classroom.

Intentionality, like changing our classroom setup, included interior design and, most importantly, the materials for children to learn and explore. And so one Saturday, we decided to meet up in the classroom and meticulously rearranged the classroom. Although we had already drawn a plan in one of our meetings, in actual fact, we still found changes that needed to be executed. The materials and furniture that we needed to keep or get rid of had been a debate too. But because it was discussed with clear objectives and reasons, we came to a unified decision. The classroom environment received a lot of commendations from coworkers, families, and, most of all, the children. The children became at ease in the room in the first few months. They became familiarized with areas and materials, and thus challenging behaviors were kept to a minimum. Consistency in teaching practice was evident and reflected in the children and their families. We opened the floor to parents by constantly communicating with them and letting them feel that their children are also our children through our constant care and love for them. Giving them information about their children's day was of key importance and not simply "They had a great day." All these things happened with our constant communication with each other verbally and through body language.

Writing the Truth

S. J. talks about the idea of real versus alive:

It is my belief that in order to teach children anything about anything, you have to know yourself first, and still the chances are that you won't have any of the "right" answers to their questions. And really . . . you don't need to know, but you do have to be willing to go the distance alongside them to find some kind of truth. I use the word truth loosely, because truth is based in perception and personal experience. Truth takes many forms and can be found in unlikely places.

We first had the notion that our children were interested in the difference between real and alive after we began collecting raw data from the children in pictorial and written form. Ideas around the concepts of real and alive initially arose after the children read a fictitious story about a mythical character called the Crustman.

Aya tells the story of how the Crustman character developed:

The first character that children discussed in depth in our classroom was Crustman. The beginning of his journey went something like this: "If you don't eat the crust on your bread, Crustman will come to your bed when you are sleeping and put crust all over your bed. You will then become itchy and cannot sleep well. The Crustman is made of crust. He is really tiny, lives on Mars, and has special gears to find your bed. Crustman wants people to not waste their food."

Last year children in the classroom created a storybook filled with Crustman pictures and stories. We shared this with the current year of children to encourage them to create their own storybook.

Instead of creating a book, however, children got really invested in the story, and they wanted to send a letter to the Crustman. To send the letter, children had to find a way to send a letter to an imaginary character. After some discussion, they came to the conclusion that Crustman would visit the locker of one particular child in the class who doesn't eat crusts. So they created letters to put in the child's locker. Everyone drew pictures, and teachers helped them to write their questions in the letter.

I took on the role of Crustman after class and wrote them a reply; once they received the reply, they believed that Crustman was real. As a team, we discussed what the Crustman would say in the letter. We all agreed that although we could write these letters, we would not answer questions that had no clear answer. For example, if they asked whether Crustman is real, we would not reply with a clear answer but rather give them space to think for themselves.

Children were really excited to see Crustman's reply and thought very carefully about what was said in the letter. At one point, children even pointed out that Crustman was actually wasting crusts by putting them on children's beds! This was a very interesting point that none of us had considered. We teachers needed to discuss our reply so that Crustman wasn't seen as wasteful. We decided that Crustman only throws out expired crust that cannot be eaten.

In total about twenty letters were exchanged between children and Crustman. Children often repeated the same questions, but we wrote them in the letter anyway. As they sent more and more letters, their questions become more complex, including the paradox I described above. It was great to see how deeply children can think, even if it's for an imaginary character.

When we started the letter project, children were not sure if Crustman was real because he didn't show up to put crust on their beds even when they didn't eat crust. They asked this question to Crustman in the letters. However, by the end of the letter-writing period, the children became sure that Crustman exists because of the replies.

We also approached children to draw Crustman, or, rather, how they imagine Crustman looked. We made a prop based on one of the children's Crustman drawings and encouraged them to create a story with it using a toy house.

Some children liked this idea and showed a strong interest in creating a Crustman house so he could stop by our school. Creating this house became a big project, and children would spend hours decorating the house.

We approached children to create Crustman using clay by first putting it on paper.

Our classroom has three groups of children, each led by one teacher. The Crustman story first started in my group of children and naturally spread to the other two. Every day teachers shared what had happened in our groups and created different activities in response. I think that when children were deeply into this character, the best thing we could do was to experiment—research—on how to best support their interest and to help their imagination grow. Crustman was our first testing stage to see which approaches work and how it affects what children do. We also tried to see how we could work as a group, even though we each had a group of our own for circle/group time. This was before we hung our sheets of papers in the classroom, as discussed below, so we just constantly discussed what was going on in the class.

B. shares some thoughts on Crustman and the children's fears:

The children believed in his existence. I knew two of my children became hard-core believers because they used to be crust haters, but they started to eat crust on bread and pizza! Also there were other children who were just afraid of his existence and believed that Crustman was bad; they wanted to "destroy" him—organically, by dipping the crust in water so it would soften and be easy to eat, or that they should remember to put him in a green bin rather than in the garbage. Children who were thinking of "violence" were not really thinking of killing him (i.e., such as what villains and superheroes might do) but the ways that they could get rid of him.

The children believed that Crustman was related to the scarecrow in our playground, the heads (busts) in the classroom, and witches. They believed that all of the characters that were built in the classroom converged at night or lived "behind the door." Trolls and aliens came to life as well. All of these thoughts occurred because we said yes to them and listened to what they had to say. We did not stop their argument nor their ideas but instead tried to create sparks by asking, "Could you tell me more about it?"

S. J. continues:

We noticed how the children in this classroom debated about the existence of this character and then how their ideas surrounding "real" and "alive" bled into various other play scenarios. The children built houses for *real* fairies, and they created elaborate stories about a scarecrow in the playground, who happens to come alive at nighttime and who conveniently, during those late hours, interacts on occasion with both the Crustman and Santa Claus. We watched as the children took time to form their arguments to support either side of the debate regarding the existence of these beings. We allowed the children to explore all of the angles without much interjection regarding our own beliefs.

Our curiosity piqued when the children began to make clear and definite decisions around classifying something as either real or alive. For example, the children explained that their families were both real and alive, but that feelings were real but not necessarily alive. We noticed how the children seemed to be struggling with the existence of abstract notions, like emotions. The children seemed to recognize that experiences that are felt but not seen are still real, which created another problem for the children to debate: that existence or the *aliveness* of something may not be able to be detected by sight. For example, two children engaged in a heated conversation around whether cars were alive because they could move and were fueled by a precious fluid, much like blood. Cars seemed to fit into the category of alive for one child but not the other because of the car's inability to talk, which seemed to be a necessary trait in order to fit into his schema. During this particular conversation, another child chimed in to say that some cars do talk, and indeed they do with modern technology. Could artificial intelligence be yet another element in the puzzle of life for children in our modern time?

It was challenging for us to hold back our own bias and to really listen to these arguments. The children were asking extremely complicated questions, bringing in thoughts about life, death, and existence in general. We believe that the children were desperately trying to find a truth that sat well with them, a truth that blends reality and mystery to create a space where anything is possible. We believe that our children were on a spiritual quest, a journey as individual as it was collective, and we believe that allowing our children to ask these questions to each other has laid a strong cultural foundation in our classroom where dialogue and experimentation are deeply valued.

Documenting This Process Was Messy–and Valuable

Aya describes a different kind of documentation, one that was "in the moment" rather than carefully prepared and beautiful:

Another way for us to express bravery was through our documentation. We documented our experiences by doing rough documentation; we let go of "making it beautiful" but carefully combined all of our thoughts together using sticky notes, rough paper, and so on.

We placed paper everywhere in the classroom for us to be able to write down our thoughts and what happened in the classroom whenever we need to, as we worked with the children or when they rested.

This also allowed us to comment on each other's notes in real time, when things are actually happening. We were being brave because the data looked messy, contrary to what is usually expected by ourselves and perhaps by those reading the work.

We didn't know how our documentation would work and look when we were writing but had to have faith that this tumble of writing would be useful. However, this process allowed us to leave our assumptions about children's thoughts at the door and write what actually happened, usually as it happened. I found that our method worked wonderfully for compiling our thoughts; in those papers are collections of thoughts from all three of us, as well as our questions and puzzles. (Because we did our documentation in real time, we really crafted this documentation together. If one person had the responsibility to do more formal documentation, it might be easy for the documentation to express only one person's view.) People usually expect a conclusion from formal documentation, and we feel that this can be a big factor in terms of missing what is really in the children's minds.

We didn't put many pictures on our documentation, but it attracted a lot of people because of the content. Children showed a lot of interest in it because they knew that their ideas were written on those sheets, exactly as they occurred.

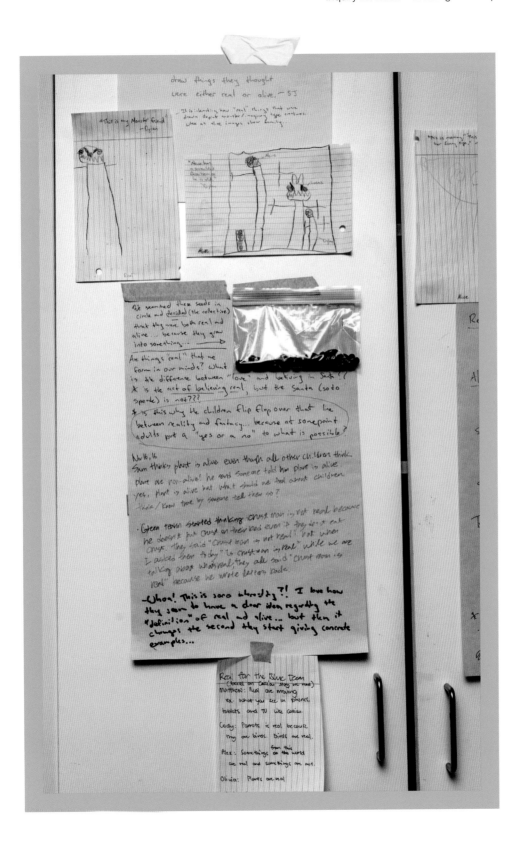

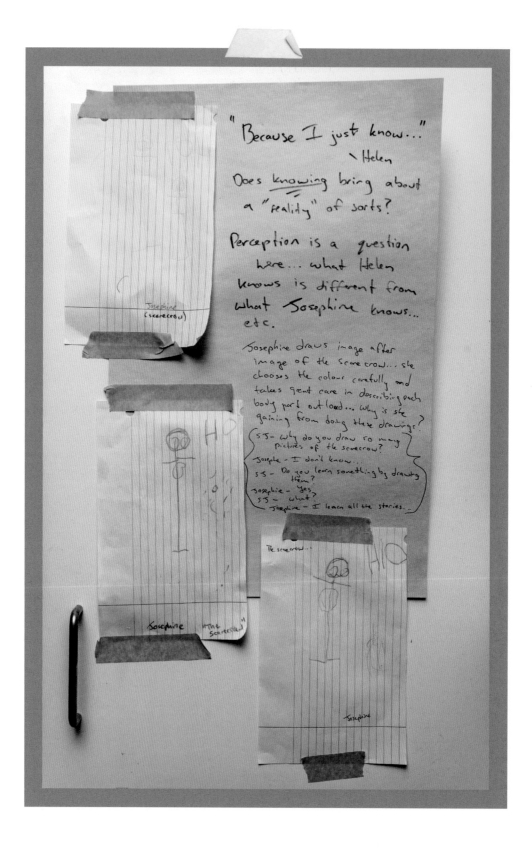

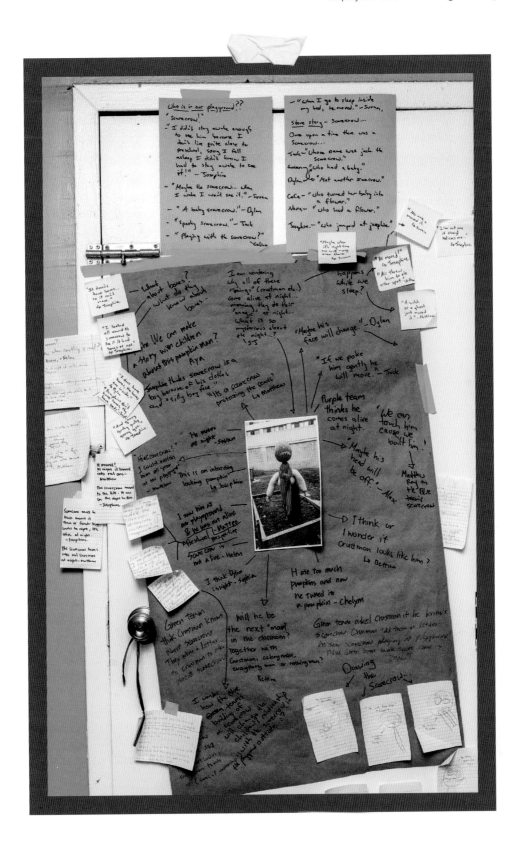

They often asked us to read what was written when they were discussing these same topics in class.

A lot of parents also showed interest in our documentation; they spent time to read it and ask questions about it. Getting parents and children's interest is always a challenge, even for beautifully crafted formal documentation, so we are proud of what we have achieved.

Teachers from other classrooms would also read and comment on our documentation.

We invited everyone come into our classroom to write what they think, freely and openly.

S. J. comments on the "messy" documentation:

We documented this huge project on our classroom walls and cupboards, simply sticking up all of the information that the children were feeding us. The classroom was overtaken with sticky notes.

Documenting in this way served many purposes for us. Our classroom is big and filled with many bodies. It can be hard to hold on to a thought, as so much is always happening at once. Putting up the information as it flowed organically allowed us to keep the momentum of this project flowing. It also helped us to keep our teaching triangle in check. We made a silent promise to each other to listen and gather as much as we could, maintaining a mindset that nothing is trivial when working with children. We wrote down everything they said in relation to ideas around real versus alive.

The children picked up on this way of showing their learning, and, in turn, they began requesting their ideas be tacked up. The children were as committed to this process as we were. They wanted to be involved; they wanted to discover. One day in particular stands out as a turning point for me in knowing that this process works. A child and I were discussing what classifies something as being a toy. I was asking her all sorts of questions, playing the devil's advocate. I asked her a series of questions about play and toys and whether adults played, to which she responded, "I don't understand you; you have to ask me another question so that I can understand." She wanted to keep the conversation flowing; she wanted more from me. She later handed me a piece of paper with drawing and writing on it. She explained that she wanted me to put it up on the wall against what I had written about our conversation, because this was her interpretation of what had happened. This was when I knew that we were doing something right. She knew her ideas were as valid as mine. She knew she had something to offer. She knew how to dig deeper. We managed to truly listen to them.

Time and Weight

S. J. discusses the project's end:

We started this monumental project in September 2016 and brought it to a close in April 2017. In that time, we often asked ourselves, "Is it over? When will we know when it's done?" However, we always left the data up just a little bit longer, just to see . . . and see we did.

New ideas continued to emerge. You could see each child's understanding of the topics becoming more complex and rich. During our team meetings, we voiced how we felt about each new thought that made its way to our wall.

We argued immensely about crossing an invisible line, one that might potentially get us into troubled spaces with our families. Letting children talk openly about death and God and aliens and ghosts puts educators into uncomfortable places, or so I felt. I was so worried that with each passing day, someone would say to me, "What are you teaching my kid?" As a team, we talked about what we should encourage and what we should discourage within these topics, and when it came down to it, our fears were rooted in our own bias and discomforts. We also wondered if the work we were doing really mattered. Did it mean anything? Did it have an effect? Again acknowledging our vulnerability and trusting in each other allowed us to ask each other these hard questions. I admitted to my coworkers that I was scared of what our families *might* say. We picked apart what we thought might be our own incentives instead of the children's. We asked ourselves, "Are we following the paths that the children create, or do we (or should we) craft the paths *with* the children?" We came to the conclusion that if we do not craft collaboratively with the children and with each other that we "will get lost if we are not careful." We decided that we should always be listening for and acting on sculptable moments. All of the time that we dedicated to debating made us realize how important our voices were in this journey—how our questions matter, and how it was our questions to each other about our intentions that in turn made us better educators in this journey alongside the children.

B. adds her thoughts about parents' perceptions:

We wondered, "What did parents think about this work and the tangents that it took? Where was their voice in the classroom?" I believe that we consistently nurtured these children through the center's and the team's philosophy, which were closely aligned. The parents did not struggle with entrusting the children to this program. They entered our Brave Space through their own opinions, observations, and experiences, which they shared with us. Our classroom was pretty diverse in terms of its population, and I appreciate that a lot of learning unfolded. This Brave Space opened up the floor to parents to feel part of their children's lives, even though they weren't physically present throughout the days—so important to parents.

Aya chimes in:

Of course it is possible for parents to have concerns, but we really won't know until we have tried and communicated our intentions. I think that sometimes we as teachers worry too much about parents' reactions, but we found that although it felt a little uncomfortable to discuss some of our inquiry topics at first, we are glad that we tried, because parents seemed to understand and enter into the inquiry. They had heard a lot from their children about these characters, and they understood why we discussed imaginary characters in class. . . . The documentation on the wall helped them to understand that we were supporting children to develop their ideas. If we had waited to develop "traditional" documentation, for it to be "finished," then parents would not have been so up to date on the topics being explored and may have worried. This is the benefit of producing "live" and rough documentation.

Asking–Keeping the Energy

S. J. comments more on their process:

We put our own ponderings and queries up on the wall as well. We asked each other clarifying questions and directionality questions. We pointed out areas of interest and words and phrases the children said that floored us. We also wrote each other small stories and even a poem or two that related to the topics. This was an avenue of communication that knew no boundaries and that allowed us to be as open and candid as we liked.

We decided not to look for an end but rather the connections within. We saw this web of intricate ideas and feelings and questions emerge before our eyes, and it was alive. It breathed in and out; it showed our frustrations, our hesitations, and our fears. We worried that it wasn't true pedagogical documentation because it wasn't pretty . . . until, of course, we realized that its appearance, with all its layers of thoughts and notions, was a perfect visualization of our collective. It was messy and huge, a lot like the feelings we shouted, laughed, and cried to each other during the making of this learning map. Other teachers added their ideas when they felt the impulse, and so did our families. We invited our entire community to engage with our children's learning through this medium.

During our asking, we discovered that we were constantly feeding the children opportunities to dive deeper by responding to their thoughts with

"Yes . . . and then what?" This kept the momentum going, another theater trick that works in the real world with real people. When studying improvisational theater, it's important to always say yes to whatever the other person is offering you in a scene so that the energy never dies. We took this idea and ran with it. We ran with it for seven months, and what we accomplished alongside our children astounds us.

Aya adds her thoughts:

By responding to their interests earnestly, teachers can give the children confidence in themselves. Our interest and careful listening tells them that we value what they think and respect their thoughts. Children in our classroom are empowered to think things through by themselves, even though this can be uncomfortable for teachers at times. They don't simply listen and follow what we say; during an inquiry, they form their own ideas and ask lots of questions when they disagree or don't understand.

As teachers we are happy to see children develop this trait; we don't want our children to only follow what others say and believe just because they were told to. This independence and attitude will surely help them in their learning in the future.

However, this also makes our life as teachers a bit harder, since we need to reflect carefully when we ask children to do something or enter into discussions with them!

Wondering in Circles

S. J. reflects on the project:

I look back on this first year and wonder what it is that we did. Our children grew, they learned, they are all about to head off on their next big adventure, but did our mode of documentation, our focus on saying yes, and our intentional Brave Space give them any sort of advantage? We set out to collect meaningful stories, to be witnesses to children and families and to be witnessed as educators, which we also did. But still, what was the significance of it all?

We have come to realize that we encouraged the children in our care to be deep and critical thinkers. We nurtured a sense of curiosity in our children, one that always asks *why*. The children we spent the year with practiced debating and arguing with each other and with us. We asked them to step into our Brave Space and to question their peers. We validated their ideas and thoughts by adding them to our learning map, thus proving to them that their voices matter. We asked them big questions and expected big answers.

As educators we nurtured each other. We spent countless hours discussing our beliefs, our intentions, and in doing so we learned how to be *still* and *present* with each other. We were authentic, and we showed our children how vulnerable, maskless people look and feel on a daily basis. I don't think this is the end.

Reflecting on This Inquiry . . .

What strikes you about the teachers' thinking during this inquiry? What puzzles or delights or troubles you? For me, when I first heard and saw this inquiry, I was struck by the uncertainty felt by these new educators and the courage it took to overcome this uncertainty in order to move forward and deeper with the children.

Let's examine some of the major points and cognitive knots—for children and teachers—as they journeyed into their Brave Space:

- Everything began with relationship between individuals and the team as a whole. The triangle of this relationship was always respected; deep trust was built before in-depth work with the children began. In this way, everything was negotiable. There was no way of knowing at the beginning of the inquiry what would unfold. Yet the trust among team members made this feel less intimidating, and when fears did arise, there was deep dialogue and, yes, arguments until resolution was reached. B. says, "It is important in the classroom to allow yourself to learn, not only from your colleagues, but also from children and families. That makes a classroom feel like home and safe for everyone."

- From the very beginning, there was a determination to make this physical space into an intentional one—not a space inherited from someone else, in which the status quo was protected, but a space that reflected the teachers' and center's philosophy and teaching approaches, with room for the children to contribute and change the environment as needed during inquiries (for example, their work with the idea of fairies and their homes).

- There is value in exploring "risky" topics with the children. As we saw in the teachers' writing, the topics that came up caused great consternation for the team. Is it okay to explore ghosts, death, or imaginary characters that may be a little scary for some children? Throughout this exploration, there were constant discussions about this, especially since the team worried so much about parents' thinking on these topics. These families were from all over the world, holding diverse beliefs from their own cultures. The importance of documentation comes to the forefront here. All of the team members believed that the very rough documentation was non-intimidating; it invited the parents to come in and read, to keep abreast of what was being explored, and, importantly, to contribute their own thinking through adding questions and thoughts. This open and friendly communication went a long way in allaying teachers' fears and keeping parents "in the loop" of this highly imaginative world. Aya describes reactions to a conversation about ghosts: "We found this conversation wonderful until they started discussing if ghosts are real or not. We wondered if it was okay for children to discuss this topic; we thought it could be really scary for children, and it may not become a positive discussion for them. We were also worried about parents' reactions. However, when we discussed the children's conversations with parents, they didn't seem to be as concerned with it as we were! It is still scary to talk about some topics with children and parents; nevertheless, we pushed ourselves as far as we could to think about the best ways to support children."

- Over time other topics arose that might be considered "creepy." Aya explains that the children talked about zombies and witches, as well as a mannequin head that could talk when no one was looking. She says, "Supporting children's imagination stopped becoming just fun, but an uneasy thing to do. For me, it was hard to understand if this was a sensitive topic, or not, for Canadians. It was hard for me to imagine how the families felt, and I'm still wondering why parents were not worried about these topics when we explained it to them."

- Aya raises a good point. Why were parents not concerned? We can only speculate that they considered their children to be in a very psychologically safe place with these teachers. Great care was taken to listen to all children and to honor their thinking and their imagination, to listen to conversations that in other circumstances might have been discouraged or even forbidden. This brings us to the big question of the role of the teacher and our image of the child.

- Throughout this inquiry, we see not only the child's voice but also the teacher's. At times, teachers stepped in to sustain the inquiry or add intrigue, such as letters from Crustman. The inquiry became, then, a two-way conversation between teachers and children, with each contributing. Great care was taken, however, not to provide answers for children but to allow them to come to their own conclusions. Aya says, "Because we let children explore these ideas in depth, they showed a strong ability to think for themselves." B. adds, "We called it a Brave Space for a lot of reasons. We allowed them to say whatever they needed to say and respected their opinions. We journeyed with them in their imaginary world while also thinking about what their parents thought about all this."

- This view of how to be with children and how to go to previously unexplored topics depicts the team's image of the child as capable and full of potential, ideas, and theories.

- We see that throughout this inquiry, there was much questioning and curiosity on the part of the teachers. They allowed themselves to "not know" and embrace the disequilibrium that this created. The eventual feelings of accomplishment, of learning through this experience, came from documentation of not only what was happening on a day-to-day basis, but also from including their questions and their wonderings, declaring their vulnerability, and allowing others to enter their space and offer their own opinions and questions. In this way, the inquiry became a shared experience, a true collaboration among all the protagonists. B. says, "We became confident in sharing our opinions and thoughts. We found our cultures and value systems and beliefs settled into our Brave Space without the feeling of being judged or questioned. This allowed us to get to know each other and appreciate our differences, which made us even more consistent in the classroom."

- Throughout this inquiry, the teachers had the support of a pedagogical consultant, Liz Hicks, who you will remember talked about the nature of her work in a previous chapter. Within this inquiry, Liz's role—according to the teaching team—was to listen to their challenges, ask thought-provoking questions, provide encouragement, and facilitate critical thinking. Not all early childhood settings have the benefit of such a person to scaffold their thinking, but it has become a priority for this center to budget for this type of support. The director of this child care organization, Susan Willis, has always supported staff growth and innovation and has kept these values in mind as she budgets for staff support.

- If it is not available to you, then a master teacher (someone with significant expertise and knowledge) or a representative from a local resource center can often fill this role. Communities of practice can also fill the role of cothinker in this situation.

- At the beginning of this story of inquiry, there is a quote from S. J.: "Learning to be still and present have been two of the most meaningful tools that I have used in my experience as being a witness to another person's story."

- Being "still and present" is indeed an important tool, one that we should be using whether listening to children or colleagues. This inquiry is a testament to the power of careful listening, deep reflection, and thoughtful response.

Final Reflections and an Invitation

What would happen if we liberated ourselves, along with the children we teach, from old scripts? What would a classroom look like if it revolved around children's investigations, ideas, struggles, and successes, and what if all these aspects were all clearly visible? And what if we developed curriculum around not only these ideas but also our own values in terms of teaching and learning?

Inquiry can be liberating—not free from accountability, expectations from society, or our administrations, but free from rigidity, a "production-line" mode of thinking, and outdated models of teaching and learning. While meeting the requirements of our societal systems, it is possible, as we have seen from examples in this book, to create an environment where verbs such as *engaging*, *wondering*, *questioning*, *trying*, and *retrying* describe our way of being with young children.

Pam Oken-Wright (2017), in her online article "The Child's Right to Try," writes,

> I've been thinking lately about the right of children to "try." So much of data-driven, test-apprehensive pedagogy has set the shared value at the right answer. Failure is to be avoided at all costs. If they can't pass the standardized test, push more, push harder. And the child's right to The Try disappears. Deep in him is a fear of failure and, consequently, either untenable stress or a coping mechanism or two that allow the child to say he doesn't care.
>
> What if we introduced The Try into the curriculum? What if teachers were encouraged to imagine and construct opportunities for The Try in their early childhood (0-8 yrs) classrooms? What if teachers themselves discovered their own right to try?

Inquiry gives both teacher and child a right to try—to walk alongside one another, learning and changing together, co-constructing and collaborating, and wondering about the world and how it works. We live in a world where knowledge is constantly changing, and to know how to ask, search, and try is vitally important for not only children but also for teachers too.

The nature of a play-based, emergent program is to inquire, probe, experiment, and mess about. Through this process, we encounter unexpected delights, develop our own theories about how children learn and how we might teach, and, if we are observant and vigilant, arrive at the questions and ideas of children which—when taken seriously—will lead to deeper learning through engagement.

It takes time to work in this way. For newcomers this means it takes time to learn about this approach and reflect upon what it might mean for you. What do you believe? What are your values around children's learning, and how might you work with those values in mind? For seasoned educators, thinking through the process of inquiry-based learning and the environments that support it might be provocative: What are the possibilities? What are some small steps that you could take toward action? What are your questions, and how will you find the answers to them in the context of your daily life with children? This may be *your* inquiry.

I invite you to wonder and to wander along with children and to weave your beliefs and values into your environment, to make inquiry a way of life . . . living, breathing, and changing.

Appendix

Loose Parts and Intelligent Playthings Categorized by Schema

If your child loves:	(S)He may be exploring	Loose Parts	Natural Loose Parts
Train sets, buckles, Lego, harnesses, fridge magnets, stickers, marker caps, shoes	Connecting	Popsicle sticks, matchsticks, golf tees, paper clips, binder rings, carabiners, felt pieces, tissue paper pieces, elastics, fabric, paper, burlap, balsa wood, sticky notes, labels, glow-stick bracelets, pipe cleaners, belts, Velcro hair rollers, corks, pins, box rivets, screws, nails, binder clips, spring snaps, bolt snaps	Earth magnets, roots, ground pine, vines, spruce sap (for glue), beggar_ticks, burdocks, sweet gum balls, cicada shells, thistle flowers, leather cord, dandelion stems (for chains), dried bones, wet leaves, sand, snow, ice
Cutting with scissors, knocking towers down, making playdough into small segments, tearing pages from books, taking apart electronics or devices, destroying objects, removing couch cushions, cutting hair	Disconnecting/ Deconstructing	String, paper, tissue paper, cardboard, balsa wood, floral foam, Styrofoam blocks, dominoes, glow sticks, water beads, balloons, evaporated cornstarch water (for cracking), colored tape for peeling and cutting	Brittle sticks, dead branches, peeling bark, leaves, daisies, mushrooms, ice puddles and other ice forms, dry mud, clamshells, cobwebs, dried lavender, catkins, sandstone, pinecones, seedpods, coconuts, slate rock, lumps of brown sugar, fungus, cattails, dried herbs, flowers, food items for cutting and peeling
Airplanes, car crashes, balls, sharks, birds, Superman, throwing toys, throwing food, jumping off things, knocking things down, expressive art, basketball, bubbles, explosions	Trajectory	Paper, pom-poms, rubber bands, balloons, corks, beanbags, spoons, rulers, Ping Pong balls, string, ribbons, cotton balls, felt balls, Koosh balls, pieces of foam, sponges, pillows, boards and cylinders (for catapults), teapot, watering can, homemade pipe cannon for balls	Helicopter pods, feathers, leaves, flat rocks for skipping, stones for tossing into water, sticks, pinecones, Y-shaped branches (for slingshot), swinging vines, live insects, cottonwood fluff, dandelions, bursting wild snapdragon pods, snowballs, sticks as fishing poles, palm branches

Large Play	Recyclable/ Repurposed	Additional Tools/ Bases	Commercial Toys/ Gifts *
Log rounds or stumps for stacking, tires, boards, wooden spools, webbing, lumber, pallets, logs, ropes and carabiners	Containers with lids, bread clips, PVC pipes, nuts and bolts, electrical wires, Marettes, twist ties, buckles and snaps from discarded items, Velcro from old clothes, broccoli elastics, straws	Hammer, tape, glue, twine, rope, yarn, bungee cords, hooks, chains, cable ties, latches and fasteners, tongs, webbing, flannel, stapler, safety pins, contact paper, magnetic surface, corkboard	K'NEX, gear sets, slot-a-shape builders, magnet builders, Unifix cubes, Ring-a-ma-jigs, GoldieBlox, Straws and Connectors, Bristle Blocks, Magneatos, puzzles, Snap Circuits, Brik-a-Blok, Mecanno Junior, train sets, Barrel of Monkeys, snap-together beads
Giant cardboard boxes, haystacks, snowbanks, balloons, sand, stacks of tissue boxes	Telephone books for stacking and knocking over, magazines for cutting, egg cartons, bubble wrap, crushable cans and bottles, corks, used electronics, knitted articles to unravel	Mortar and pestle, safety knives, safety scissors, hammer, clippers, pliers, mallet, saw, screwdrivers, hole punches, flyswatters	Battat Take-Apart sets, toy demolition vehicles, Silly Putty, excavation kits, magnet builders, Unifix cubes, wooden block sets, "Thin Ice" game, "Scratch Magic" art
Planks, cable spool, skate ramp, platforms, ladder, chairs, yoga ball, slide, sled, rain gutters, a pair of trees and physio band for giant slingshot, pliable birches (for swinging), pool noodles	Pipes, scarves, plastic bottles (for rockets), paper towel tubes, broccoli elastics, springs, plastic spoons, buckets for ball toss, boxes for crash zone, inner tubes, film canisters, boxes and cartons for knocking down	Hammers, saws, mortar and pestle, targets, hoops, mini zip lines, fans, launchpad, balcony, antacids and vinegar for rockets or "pop the top," open field or water for throwing natural loose parts	Hot Wheels tracks, catapult kit, marble run, trebuchet kit, construction sets with ramps, rocket building kits, boomerang, propeller toys, Frisbees, kites, Skyrocopter, Stomp Rockets, Micro Shotz, soda rockets, "Perfection" game

If your child loves:	(S)He may be exploring	Loose Parts	Natural Loose Parts
Forts, hide-and-seek, putting toys to bed, burying items in sand, wrapping presents, eggs and nests, hats, being inside cupboards, painting entire canvas, Lego enclosures	**Enclosing/ Enveloping**	Scarves, fabric, lace, towels, boxes, spools, paper towels, tissue paper, mailer tubes, solo cups, aluminum foil, foam pieces, folding steamer basket, plastic Easter eggs, locks and keys, hinges, hair rollers, sponges, nesting baskets, tissue paper, ribbons, yarn, plaster cloth, cheesecloth, toilet paper, Claycrete papier mâché, Paperclay	Piles of leaves, sand, mud, clay, walnut halves, clamshells, pine spills, dirt, palm branches, geodes, seedpods, flowers, petals, straw, pea stone, twigs, nests, hollow logs, leather hides, birch bark, hollowed or halved coconut shells, pumpkins, gourds, lotus pods, corn husks, giant leaves
Elevators, balls, towers, dropping objects on purpose, scribbling up and down, building tall towers	**Dynamic Vertical**	Scarves, beanbags, pom-poms, cushions, string, rope, spools, beads, foam balls, Ping-Pong balls, corks, wire, watering can, teapot, Slinky, confetti, blocks for stacking, spools, paper clips, dice, dominoes, light switches, chains, springs, barrel bolts	Rocks for stacking, pinecones, water, feathers, sticks, helicopter pods, leaves, acorns, crab apples, hanging vines, icicles, palm branches, wood pieces for stacking
Speed racers, traffic, running laps, trains, scribbling left and right, tennis, bowling, clapping, waving flags, vacuums, lawn mowers, tunnels, pushing strollers, building roads, shakers, swordplay	**Dynamic Horizontal**	Balls, marbles, level blocks for making roads, ribbons, wooden rings, rain gutters, clotheslines and clothespins, streamers, wires, strings, beads, half-pipes, elastics	Logs, trenches in the sand, branches and palm fronds, pliable branches for building tunnels, sand and streams, timothy hay, flat rocks or ice chunks for launching, chestnuts, waste apples

Large Play	Recyclable/ Repurposed	Additional Tools/ Bases	Commercial Toys/ Gifts *
Cardboard boxes, stacks of tires, tents, long tree limbs (for forts), blankets, tarps, tables, chairs, couch cushions, pallets, cylindrical concrete forms, plastic culverts, haystacks, ball pit	Fabric remnants, old hats and shawls, belts, watches, plastic containers, cups, electrical wire, cardboard tubes, egg cartons, envelope discards from card stores, wrapping paper, newsprint, magazines, bubble wrap	Clothespins, safety pins, rubber bands, string, tape, Velcro tape, twist ties, magnifying glass, washi tape, Mod Podge, Silly Putty	MagnaTiles, Russian nesting dolls, stacking cups, Lego, Brik-a-Blok, Crazy Forts, sleeping bag, igloo mold, skipping rope, mosaic kit, piggy bank, piñata, doll clothes, latch board, hollow blocks, mailbox, excavation kit
Stacks of tires, platforms, chairs, ladders, walls, tree trunks, fences, couch cushions, cylindrical concrete forms, trampoline, dumbwaiter, fireman pole, deep hole, water pump	PVC pipes, wrapping paper tubes, Pringles chip containers, K-Cups, yogurt cups, cans, zippers, tissue boxes, Yop bottles, Solo cups, empty boxes, straws, coiled telephone cords	Plumb line, retractable tape measure, pulleys and ropes with bucket, small hand winch, mashers, mortar and pestle, funnel, turkey baster, hourglass, thermometer	Connect 4, stacking toys, hammer and peg set, bead maze, toy elevator, parachute men, rocket kits, skipping rope, ball & jacks, trampoline, OgoDisk, Micro Shotz, Stomp Rockets, Jacob's ladder
Logs, Hula-Hoops, culvert pipes, shallow ditches, planks, four-by-fours, curbs, stepping stones, rain gutters, concrete forms, balls and bottles for bowling, parachute, shopping cart, skateboard, stroller, wheelbarrow, bike, hockey stick, golf club	Pipes, wrapping paper tubes, rubber bands, inner tubes, physio bands, bearings, wheels, corrugated roofing	Level tables, hardwood floors, long cardboard boxes, fences or pallets for attaching gutters and pipes, preattached horizontal cables or lines, slingshot	Hot Wheels, train sets, push toys, abacus, windup toys, ride-on toys, marble run, sports equipment, air hockey table

If your child loves:	(S)He may be exploring	Loose Parts	Natural Loose Parts
Putting trucks upside down, turning knobs on stereo and appliances, planets, baseball, racetracks, CDs, launching toys that roll, spinning in circles, washing machines	**Rotation/ Circularity**	Jacks, plates, pot lids, wood rings, spools, washers, metal rings, rope, string, lasso, sticks, toilet plungers, paper towel holders, cylindrical blocks, short lengths of pipe, nuts and bolts, screws, martini umbrellas, metal bearings, mixing spoons, whisks, hair rollers, loops of tubing or pipes, serger spools, bobbins, paint roller, hinges	Helicopter pods, swinging vines, star anise, roly-polies, daisies, snowballs, tree rounds with a center hole, acorns, snail shells, coconut shells, water, stepping stones or stumps arranged in a circle, hills for rolling down
Making holes in things, poking with sticks, putting fingers in holes, arrows and bullets, swords, ice fishing, sewing, earrings, destroying safety gates, putting limbs through bars of railings	**Going through a boundary**	Yarn and plastic needles, birthday candles, dowels, craft sticks, fabric, burlap, mesh, lace, pipe cleaners, oasis, cork, golf tees, toothpicks, matchsticks, beads, buttons, chopsticks, keys and locks, bolts and boards with holes, screws, balsa wood, pins, colander, plastic canvas, screening, perforated steel containers, napkin rings, latches, hooks, Wiffle ball, artificial plants, floral foam, martini picks, C&C grid, tulle	Feathers, reeds, cattails, stems, sticks in mud, sticks in snow, bark with woodpecker holes, clay, mud, old-man's beard, tree slices with drilled holes, cracked rocks, ice and tools, ice and salt, pine tree needles, moss patches, rotting stumps, wood chips, shark teeth, shells with holes, pumpkin, gourds, perforated limestone, spiderwebs, sandstone, lotus pods, cork
Drawing around the edge of paper, walking the perimeter of a playground or building, tracing, winding string around objects, tying knots, walking over or around obstacles, bracelets and necklaces, weaving, finger knitting	**Going around a boundary**	String, tape, marbles, tubes, spools, ribbons, cups, strings of beads, ropes, wire, Popsicle sticks, pipe cleaners, elastics, blocks for building bridges and walls, blue rocks or fabric for moat-making, chains, chalk, gears and belts, floral tape, measuring tape, metal "bendy snake," C&C grid	Twigs, stumps, stepping stones, stepping stumps, roots, ivy, vines, creepers, hemp, branches, small trees, antlers, pinecones, ground pine, roots, driftwood, sand and water for moats, whelk egg casing, seaweed

Large Play	Recyclable/ Repurposed	Additional Tools/ Bases	Commercial Toys/ Gifts *
Cylindrical concrete form, plastic culvert pipes, swings, cable spools, round hay bales, freestanding poles and trunks for circling, Hula-Hoop, pop-up hamper or tunnel, merry-go-round, barrel, hose reel, Archimedes screw	Cylindrical containers, paper tubes, old microwave trays/tracks, bottles, casters, motors, knobs off old appliances, Rollerblade wheels & bolts, cups, spinners from board games, turntable, round cardboard from frozen pizza, paper plates, bobbins	Large round bowls, steel drum, fan, compasses, winch, pottery wheels, lazy Susan, rotating organizer, salad spinner, dowels and sticks, hamster wheel, clothes for toy washing machine, drill, screwdriver, auger, mixer, blender	Snap Circuits, train circuit, gear toys, bead maze, spiral ball run, abacus, Magneatos, tops, toy cement mixer, propeller flyers, skipping rope, water wheel, Spirograph, Euler's Disk, Gearation magnets, spin art, rock tumbler
Lattice, fencing, soil, sand, shovels, picks, hoes, augers, knotty pine boards, milk crates, posthole diggers, pegboards, loosely knit blankets, wine rack, windows, ladders, tunnel, parachute, finish lines, swinging doors, leaf strainer for gutters	Pieces of Styrofoam packaging, foam insulation, cardboard boxes, bits of grid wire, chicken wire, tomato cages, birdcages, carpet pieces, paper tubes, straws, bits of discarded shirts with buttons and buttonholes, bubble wrap, wire, twist tiles, rope, elastics, pegboard, industrial waste sheets with holes from punched-out objects	Hammer, drill, screwdriver, rubber mallet, tent pegs, tweezers, pliers, hole punches, shape punches, brads, spades, hand drills, weeding tools, dibbers, skewers, nutcrackers, stapler, cookie cutter, fork, garlic press, lemon juicer, tracing wheel	Honey Bee Tree game, Kerplunk, peg stackers, hammer and peg set, weaving loom, Lite-Brite, Mr. Potato Head, lacing toys, rug hooking kit, stretchy mouse-and-cheese toy
Pylons, cable spools, freestanding poles and trunks for circling, Hula-Hoop, merry-go-round, barrel, tetherball, bridges, balance beam, trees, banks and boulders for circumnavigating, bungee cords, thick ropes	Paper towel tubes, chicken wire, dye-sub printer ribbon, rubber bands, panty hose or balloons cut into rings, flexible tubing, dryer vent hose, dish drying (peg) rack, necklace and ring holders	Pegboard or nail board, loom, clusters of trees, poles or columns, hedgerows, winches and pulleys, hat tree, peg racks	Spirograph, stencils, string art set, circuit sets, maze toys, yo-yo, string top, diabolo, friendship bracelet kits, weaving kits, plush snake, race car track, Slinky, Plinko board

If your child loves:	(S)He may be exploring	Loose Parts	Natural Loose Parts
Having hands full of objects, full pockets, filling and dumping, dump trucks, bags, shopping carts, wheelbarrows	**Transporting**	Glass gems, beads, pom-poms, marbles, tiles, clothespins, nuts and bolts, washers, cotton balls, ball bearings, magnets, pails, bags, baskets, tins, fanny pack, containers, backpack, bindle stick, plastic counters, tiddlywinks, Popsicle sticks, sponges, erasers, buttons, spools, dice, chains, felt balls, cotton swabs, Styrofoam shapes, confetti, foam craft shapes, figurines, caps	Wood pieces, tree cookies, seeds, acorns, rocks, shells, leaves, pinecones, crab apples, beans, wood chips, driftwood, sand, flowers, dirt, gravel, fruits, rice, peach pits, cherry pits, deer corn, feathers, seedpods, sticks, hollowed coconut shells, sticks, branches, natural woven baskets
Putting toys in a row, arranging food on a plate, parking toy cars, sorting, sequencing by size, arranging furniture, straightening rows of shoes, stacking books	**Ordering/ Positioning**	Dominoes, birthday candles, magnets, buttons, Popsicle sticks, pom-poms, spools, beads, clothespins, matchsticks, checkers, poker chips, dice, chains, books, playing cards, washers, napkin rings, hex nuts, glass gems, tiddlywinks, paint stirrers, dowels, tiles, wooden cubes, graph paper, shoes, moulding corners, tile spacers, wooden geometric shapes	Smooth rocks, slate, sticks, logs, tree slices, stumps, acorns, beans, seeds, pods, flat leaves, crab apples, pinecones, dry bones, shells, coconut halves, snowballs, ice cubes, kindling, branches for "planting" in rows
Makeovers, body paint, fashion dolls, fantasy, mermaids, robots, shape-shifters, werewolves, costumes, mixing media, decorating, drawing on oneself, weather and sky, cooking, intentional mess making	**Transforming**	Scarves, clothespins, hair rollers, string, yarn, ribbons, wire, Mardi Gras beads, pipes, chicken wire, beads, gems, pins, sequins, buttons, picture frames, paint chip cards, bingo chips, prisms, bottles of layered liquids, water beads, shaving cream, body paint, hair rollers, elastics, plaster cloth, ice molds, soap suds, battery-operated Christmas lights, googly eyes	Water, clay, sand, leaves, mud, flowers, weeds, dried herbs, dry goods, pinecones in water, tree needles, polishing stones, peeling bark, feathers, wood pieces, branches, sticks, vines, rocks for painting, pea gravel, seeds, old man's beard, mushrooms

Large Play	Recyclable/ Repurposed	Additional Tools/ Bases	Commercial Toys/ Gifts *
Wheelbarrow, yard cart, barrel, shopping cart, large backpack, sack, wagon, sled, stroller, laundry basket, trolleys, dollies, carts, ride-on toys, cardboard box	Plastic containers, buckets, cardboard boxes, Easter baskets, reusable grocery bags, milk jugs, milk crates, used purses, cloth sacks, corks, rubber bands, bread ties, caps, corks	Scoops, tongs, funnel, shovel, spade, tool belt, clips, pulleys, clothesline, carabiners, hooks, skateboards, felt pads for furniture	Hungry Hungry Hippos, toy cargo vehicles, diggers, dump trucks, Trunki, lunch boxes, backpack, mini shopping cart, mini wheelbarrow, wagon, ride-on toy with storage, bike basket, mini figures, toy garage with elevator, toy boats
Large hollow blocks, crates, cable spools, pallets, bricks, cardboard boxes, furniture, ladders, barrels, branches, tires, logs, cords of wood, stepping stones, Twister	Bread bag clips, cups, nesting cups, leftover kitchen/bath tiles, taped-up boxes, empty bottles, sensory bottles, cardboard tubes, K-Cups, Solo cups, tissue boxes, paint swatches, plastic subfloor or silicone pyramid mat (hole side up)	Mirrors, empty frames, tray with ledge, flat bottomed cake pans, shallow boxes, ice cube trays, light box, yardstick, muffin tins, T square, level, ruler, equal arm scales, plumb line, geometry set	Snap Circuits, Froebel Gift sets, tangrams, Lego, Jenga, geometric shape builders, inset puzzles, wooden pegboard toys, mosaic kits, bowling set, nesting dolls, CitiBlocs, Katamino blocks, KAPLA, KEVA, Rush Hour game, dinky cars, parking garage
Wood pallets, mud kitchen, landscaping tools, rake, shovel, loose bricks, large cardboard boxes, paint rollers	Styrofoam heads, fabric remnants, boxes, paper tubes, binder clips, wrapping paper, old clothes, jewelry, egg cartons, cheese wax, empty K-Cups, bread tabs, elastics, rubber bands, twist ties, fashion dolls or plastic toys with faces/ paint removed	Mirrors, Plexiglas, spatulas, rakes, mixing spoons, squeeze bottles, spray bottles, mashers, mortar and pestle, rolling pin, cake pans, light table, plastic bin, water basin, flashlight, magnifying glass	Mr. Potato Head, doll clothes, building sets, Lite-Brite, MagnaTiles, Light & Color kits, thermal reactive toys, Plasticine, Creature Builders, rock tumbler, Color and Cuddle washable toys, Shrinky Dinks

If your child loves:	(S)He may be exploring	Loose Parts	Natural Loose Parts
Climbing everything, playing peekaboo games, sitting upside down, hanging from bars, looking through holes and transparent objects, standing on toys, crawling under tables, optical illusions, magic	**Orientation/ Perspective**	Mirror tiles, convex and concave mirrors, cardboard tubes, boards, stools and chairs, ropes, washers, prisms, marbles, tiddlywinks, stained glass, small figurines, scale models, empty picture frames, colored acrylic	Hay bales, reflective pools, sand, piles of leaves, large rocks, stumps, logs, coconut halves, snow, sand
Combining multiples of same objects, making finely detailed art, mosaics or collage, making confetti, harvesting, scooping and filling, ball pits, record breaking, unusual weather events, statistics, lists, textiles, layering or polishing, assembly lines, shops, merchandise displays, patterns, making tall towers or deep holes, knitting or crochet	**Aggregating/ Cumulative effect**	Sticky notes, Popsicle sticks, pins, tiles, tiddlywinks, beads, wooden cubes, aggregated magnets, poker chips, stacks of cups, balloons, gems, colored string, beach glass, found objects sorted by color, tissue paper squares, matchsticks, dice, hair rollers, sequins, ball-head pins, dried flowers, flat marbles, papier mâché, plaster, wax, Unifix cubes, math counters	Seeds, shells, shark teeth, pebbles, burdocks, chestnuts, berries, dried flowers, tree rounds, wildflowers (for bouquets), rocks, berries, pinecones, acorns, lotus pods, honeycomb or old wasp nest, sand, snow, mud, piles of leaves, sandstone, wool roving for felting, sticks of uniform length, polished stones, beach glass, straw for weaving
Shaking, banging or tapping objects, musical instruments, crinkly paper, music, rhythm and rhyme, shouting into cups or tubes, animal sounds, noisy appliances	**Sound**	Straws, tubes, funnel, pipes, balloons, buttons, beads, bells, wind chimes, dowels, marbles, tins, PVC pipes, washers, pots and pans, metal utensils, sandpaper blocks, cups, chains, corduroy, cheese grater, bobby pins, glasses of water, paint stir sticks, wrenches, wire whisk, paper plates, comb, brush, bottle of toothpicks, clay pots	Pebbles, tiny shells, beans, bamboo shoots, hollow branches, coconut shells, walnut shells, conch shell with the apex cut off, seedpods, hollow gourds, blade of grass (hold between thumbs and blow for whistle effect), driftwood, crickets

Large Play	Recyclable/ Repurposed	Additional Tools/ Bases	Commercial Toys/ Gifts *
Plastic culvert pipe, large concrete form, ladders, stools, rope hammock, Lycra sling, jungle gym, tree house, cave, barrel, Twister game, large felled tree, cornstalks, trees for climbing	Telephone books for stacking/climbing, overturned buckets, PVC pipes, CDs, sunglasses, transparent bottles, old maps, coffee cans, dental mirrors, sunglasses, colored lenses, everyday objects cut open or turned inside out	Mats for laying on, puppet theater, magnifying glass, compass, loupe, flashlights, shovels, hangers and hooks (for building downward), overhead projector	Brik-a-Blok, Crazy Forts, stilts, microscope, telescope, camera, binoculars, periscope, pop-out tunnel, tent, jungle gym, kaleidoscope, sky projector, 3-D puzzles, rocking horse, magic kit, fly-eye replicator, acrylic blocks
Stacks of tires or logs, planks, fallen branches, trunks for fort building, facing mirrors, room full of chairs to arrange, trunk cut into rounds, stacks of milk crates, stacks of Hula-Hoops, bricks, pallets	Bottle caps, bread bag clips, backsplash tiles, K-Cups, corks, CDs (broken for mosaic tiles), toilet paper tubes, marker caps, cheese wax, industrial waste products in large quantities, nuts and bolts, twist ties, anything that can be collected in large amounts	Canvas, grout, clay, cement, measuring tools, timers, mirrors, camera, mesh, grid wire, grid paper, resin or Mod Podge, glue, mortar and pestle, floral foam, flower press, containers for collecting	Bunchems, KEVA/ KAPLA / CitiBlocs, craft kits (cross-stitch, rug hooking, friendship bracelets, etc.), snow-block molds, origami paper, paint by number, rainbow loom, Perler beads, wool roving for felting, Lego, collectables
Hollow logs, garbage cans, oil buckets, fence posts and sticks, echoey stairwells, Hula-Hoop, skipping rope, pogo stick, yoga ball, two-by-fours made into a giant xylophone, large garbage bins, corrugated roofing	Bottle caps, plastic easter eggs (for shakers), rubber bands, pipes, cardboard tubes, corrugated materials, plastic water bottles, mason jar lids, pie plates, vacuum cleaner tubing, plastic buckets, tennis ball cans, yogurt containers, bubble wrap, gloves with washers and buttons attached to the fingers, metal measuring tape	Earmuffs (for other children), audio recorders, microphone, megaphone, stethoscope, speakers, computer or tablet	Zube Tube, musical instruments, metal Slinky, rainstick, Makey Makey, slide whistle, Euler's Disk, gong, percussion toys from around the world, noisemakers, Boomwhackers

Excerpted with permission from Michelle Thornhill, © 2015.

References

Avery, Jason, Karyn Callaghan, and Carol Ann Wien. 2016. *Documenting Children's Meaning: Engaging in Design and Creativity with Children and Families.* Worcester, MA: Davis Publications.

Csikszentmihalyi, Mihaly. 1996. *Creativity: Flow and the Psychology of Discovery and Invention.* New York: HarperCollins.

DeViney, Jessica, Sandra Duncan, Sara Harris, Mary Ann Rody, and Lois Rosenberry. 2010. *Inspiring Spaces for Young Children.* Lewisville, NC: Gryphon House.

Fraser, Susan, and Carol Gestwicki. 2002. *Authentic Childhood: Exploring Reggio Emilia in the Classroom.* Albany, NY: Delmar.

Fynes, Laurel. 2014. "The Fourth Teacher . . . Is Time." *The Kindergarten Life* (blog). August 7. http://thiskindylife.blogspot.ca/2014/08/the-fourth-teacher-is-time.html.

Henderson, Barbara, Daniel R. Meier, Gail Perry, and Andrew J. Stremmel. 2012. "The Nature of Teacher Research." *Voices of Practitioners* 1–7.

Hill, Lynn T., Andrew J. Stremmel, and Victoria R. Fu. 2005. *Teaching as Inquiry: Rethinking Curriculum in Early Childhood Education.* Boston: Pearson.

James, Thomas. 1983. "Teacher of Teachers, Companion of Children: An Interview with David Hawkins." *Phi Delta Kappan* 64, no. 5 (January): 362–65.

Johns, Sandy, and Jennifer Kemp. 2017. "What Makes Something Beautiful?" *Innovations* 24, no. 3 (September): 30–43.

Jones, Elizabeth, and Gretchen Reynolds. 1992. *The Play's the Thing: Teachers' Roles in Children's Play.* New York: Teachers College Press.

Kondo, Marie. 2014. *The Life-Changing Magic of Tidying Up: The Japanese Art of Decluttering and Organizing*. New York: Ten Speed Press.

Lynch, Mary, Lauren Foster Schaffer, and Ellen Hall. 2009. "Reflections on Science: The Development of the Hawkins Room for Messing about with Materials and Ideas." *Exchange* (November/December): 53–6.

Oken-Wright, Pam. 2017. "The Child's Right to Try." *The Voices of Children Blog* (blog). October 31, 2017. http://pokenwright.com/blog/the-childs-right-to-try.

Paley, Vivian Gussin. 1986. "On Listening to What the Children Say." *Harvard Educational Review* 56, no. 2 (May): 122–131.

Piven, Hanoch. 2012. "Living in a Playful Collage: Hanoch Piven at TEDxJerusalem." Filmed December 2012 in Jerusalem, Israel. TEDx video, 16:02. https://www.youtube.com/watch?v=6e99DuPQ6j8.

Prescott, Elizabeth. 2008. "The Physical Environment: A Powerful Regulator of Experience." *Exchange* (March/April): 34–7.

Rinaldi, Carlina. 2006. *In Dialogue with Reggio Emilia: Listening, Researching and Learning*. New York: Routledge.

Robinson, Ken, and Peter Gray. 2015. *Play*. Goodtastic Films. https://vimeo.com/142819446.

Stacey, Susan. 2011. *The Unscripted Classroom: Emergent Curriculum in Action*. Saint Paul, MN: Redleaf Press.

———. 2018. *Emergent Curriculum in Early Childhood Settings: From Theory to Practice*. 2nd ed. Saint Paul, MN: Redleaf Press.

Vecchi, Vea. 2012. "The Atelier: For a Richer and More Comprehensive Knowledge of New Cultural Visions." *Innovations* 19 (4): 2–7.

Warden, Claire. 2012. *Nature Kindergartens and Forest Schools: An Exploration of Naturalistic Learning within Kindergartens and Forest Schools.* Auchterarder, Scotland: Mindstretchers.

Wenger, Etienne, Richard McDermott, and William Snyder. 2002. *Cultivating Communities of Practice: A Guide to Managing Knowledge.* Boston: Harvard Business School Press.

Wien, Carol Anne, ed. 2008. *Emergent Curriculum in the Primary Classroom: Interpreting the Reggio Emilia Approach in Schools.* New York: Teachers College Press.

Williams-Siegfredsen, Jane. 2017. *Understanding the Danish Forest School Approach: Early Years Education in Practice.* New York: Routledge.

Index